THE ACCESS TO SUBJECTIVITY

THE ACCESS TO SUBJECTIVITY
Phenomenology, Buddhism, and Psychotherapy

César Ojeda

Routledge
Taylor & Francis Group

LONDON AND NEW YORK

First published 2018
by Routledge
2 Park Square, Milton Park, Abingdon, Oxon OX14 4RN

and by Routledge
711 Third Avenue, New York, NY 10017

Routledge is an imprint of the Taylor & Francis Group, an informa business

British Library Cataloguing-in-Publication Data
A catalogue record for this book is available from the British Library

Library of Congress Cataloging-in-Publication Data
A catalog record has been requested for this book

ISBN: 978-1-78220-581-4 (pbk)

Typeset in Palatino
by V Publishing Solutions Pvt Ltd., Chennai, India

Printed in the United Kingdom
by Henry Ling Limited

Special Thanks

*I want to thank the contribution and support of Drs Patricia Cordella,
Alberto Botto, and Hernán Villarino. Special recognition to Caroline
Brazier, whose books have been to me a constant source of inspiration.*

CONTENTS

ABOUT THE AUTHOR

César Ojeda is a psychiatrist and a psychotherapist and has studied philosophy at the Pontifical Catholic University of Chile. He has published numerous books on psychiatry, psychopathology, and literature as author and co-author, as well as a large number of articles on phenomenology, epistemology, philosophy, and clinical practice. His books include: *Classical Schizophrenia* (1981), *Delirium, Reality and Imagination* (1987), *The Presence of the Absent: an Essay on Desire* (1998), *The Third Stage: Critical Essays on Contemporary Psychiatry* (2003), *Martin Heidegger and the Path to Silence* (2006), *Thought and Life: Short Essays* (2006), *Karukina: the Life of Onas in Isla Grande, Tierra del Fuego* (an anthropological novel, 2006), *The Tall Woman* (a novel, 2012), *The Things of Time* (a novel, 2013), *"In Search of the Hidden Reason* (2012), and *Shaina* (a novel, 2016). All these books are published in Spanish.

INTRODUCTION

This book intends to discuss the conceptual and practical chain that allows us to understand the connection between phenomenology, Buddhism and psychotherapy. These three disciplines have completely different origins, histories, conceptualisations and academic environments and, at first blush, there seems to be no real bond between them. The thesis of this offering is that there are connections between these approaches, but they have the peculiar character of being quiet and hidden. Phenomenology and the practice of *mindfulness* have a similar, though perhaps not explicit, goal: to exclude the *ego*. Notwithstanding this connection, they approach this task from quite separate roads, each of which usually covers the goal thereby giving the impression that both disciplines are irreducible and disjoint, as if they were completely distinct and closed systems.

We maintain here that the hidden connection between these disciplines is frequently ignored, even by those who have a large and fruitful practice in each. Perhaps, in order to see the link, it is necessary to know the nodes that are connected through that link. This means that it is necessary to have one foot on each node, which is neither the interest of phenomenologists nor Buddhists. Sometimes common sense equates the *ego* or *self* (the "I" or "me" of experience) with consciousness, yet the same identification occurs in phenomenology, despite the fact that, from its original conceptual development, there is enough reason to conclude the opposite. Even the founder of phenomenology, the German philosopher and mathematician Edmund Husserl, not only fails to exclude the experiential ego in the first steps of phenomenological reduction (*epojè* in Greek), but reaffirms it as the necessary ground point from which to reach the transcendental reduction, arriving at the "transcendental ego". We will try to demonstrate here, then, that consciousness is impossible to understand if we start or end the journey grounded in the ego.

Buddhism is very much explicit and maintains that ego is the great jail, the great addiction and one of the most important sources of suffering for human beings. For this reason, mindfulness is a path that allows us to have a relationship with others and with the world in general, without the ego's interferences.

We start this little book with a theme that is difficult to grasp, which has a language and conceptual structure that is not easy to understand through superficial reading—especially for those readers who do not have a philosophical background. This arid part will be tackled in Chapters One and Two. I would have liked to have made this part easier in some way, but the nature of philosophical phenomenology precludes that possibility. Nevertheless, the only requisite to proper understanding is slow and careful reading.

From that point on, things progress fluidly and, in my view, end in an obvious vinculum of both the above-discussed disciplines and psychotherapy. Our thesis is that psychotherapists must "suspend" (or put between quotes, as it were) their egos, as this is the only way in which it is possible to see "the other". This means that the consultant must be without distortions, including theoretic and cultural ones. Nevertheless, in the course of the journey to follow, we offer a basic review of the relevant concepts and results of psychotherapeutic investigation into what we have called the "external view". In fact, the "external view" is the one that investigators use in their attempt to reduce psychotherapy to a scientific object. We propose that psychotherapy is an intimate process, impossible to carry out whilst someone is peeping through the keyhole.

CHAPTER ONE

Subjectivity

Psychiatric and psychological clinical professionals direct their activity to people who show some form of psychic suffering. Independently of the way we explain such suffering, that is to say, of the theories and assumptions we use to understand it, their activity concerns in first instance the suffering that people *experience*. And every experience occurs in the field of what is called "subjectivity". Therefore, we, psychiatrists and psychologists, have to deal with knowledge, explanation and understanding of subjectivity.

We must, then, ask ourselves what is or what we call "subjectivity". Of course it is a concept that we could address as *operational*, since we use it and we operate with it—that is, it is a concept that helps us to think—but, usually, we do not thematise and, therefore, it is a concept we rarely think *about*. In another sense, subjectivity seems to make sense as part of a polarity: the subject-object. However, to specify this polarity and to take it out from the invisibility in which it usually remains, then things get complicated. And they do so because in its origin the word "subject" comes from the prefix "sub" which in Latin means "under", "underneath" and, at the same time, it refers to the *seizure* of something (for example, by some form of authority); similarly, *subiecto* refers to "low places, valleys, as well as the submissive person." This idea of "sinking" is easily understood in English if we bring to mind words such as "subjugate", "subject" or "subordinate". But, on the other hand, *subiecto* means "to put, to put under" and possesses also the sense of what "underlies" that which more obviously appears—that is to say, it has the character of *foundation*.

For its part, *objectus* in Latin is what belongs or is related to the thing, to the "object itself", and not to our way of thinking or needing. The "object" is "dis-interested", is independent, sufficient, compact, and "dispassionate", and its existence is on the "outside" of the subject who knows, and, therefore, it can be matter of knowledge or sensitivity for it, which operates as a matter for its faculties. But, in a sense maybe less known, *objectus* is also the *thetic* action, that is, of "putting before" (here is where the known expression "thesis" comes from), but it is a putting before that obstructs, as, for example, when we "object to" this or that. If we press this concept a little further, we could say with Zubiri that the object offers us resistance, which in his philosophy is linked to what he called a thing itself, or a *real* thing (Zubiri, 1980).

However, this classic view has been, in turn, objected to by different forms of modern and contemporary epistemology, especially by Kant, by phenomenology and, not long ago, by different forms of constructivism. In the case of phenomenology, those objections began with the notion of "intentionality" coined by Brentano and widely developed by Husserl (1986). Let us remember that *intentio* is "to bridge a gap"; in this case, a bridge between the act (psychic) and its being unavoidably directed to "something". Consequently, to love is to love "something", to think is to think "something", to remember is to remember "something". That "something" is the "objective" reference of such acts of loving, wanting or thinking. In the thought of Husserl, the *Noesis* (the act) is indissolubly linked to the *Noema* (the object of those acts) and the bridge is formed by a meaning or sense. It is no longer a "subjective" entity put in contact with an "objective" entity, but the only way in which consciousness of something is constituted: the noetic-noematic complex.

The first person

With the purpose of having an initial point of reference, we can say that the first person conjugates itself as "I", an executer of verbal forms: I think, I imagine, I love. The second person is a "you", who is in front of me and relates with me, and the third, is a "her", "him" or "it" who is there, but are not now in a direct relationship with me. Francisco Varela, from the beginning of his career, thought that the "objective" world is nothing more than a construction of the experience that every living being has when connecting to an environment and acting within it according to their own structure and dynamics. There is not, therefore, a "world itself"—the reality of Zubiri—waiting "outside" to be discovered and explained, as assumed in the practice of common sense and in a great part of contemporary scientific thought.

Cognitive science authoritatively assures us that the study of consciousness (for them, a synonym for subjectivity or mind) has been mauled by philosophy and speculation, and has remained unamenable to the powers of science. What Varela and Shear (2005) (and many others) try to generate as an antidote is what they have called "methodologies in the first person", that is to say, a procedure that allows scientific access to the study of consciousness. To do so, they must negotiate a "way", a method that allows these experiences in the first person— which happen to me consciously—to enter the field of science, and in that way settle a trustable link with the more traditional objects of it, the latter obtained through methodologies described as "in the third person", which will be the object of our interest later on.

Varela understands events in the first person as lived experience associated with cognitive and mental events. The terminology of his understanding is evidently circular: "lived", "first person", "experience", "mind", "cognition" (this last term, in its Cartesian origin, is just a way of naming the experience). These terms are not explained in each other, but are basically the same. And to explain the same with the same is a tautology. For the first person, sometimes Varela also uses terms such as "phenomenological consciousness" or "qualia". The expression "qualia" is used to address phenomena that are accessible in a conscious way. For example: the roughness of a fabric under my touch, or a pain in my abdomen, or being angry, or solving a second degree equation. In all these cases I am somebody that experiences something that usually we call "subjective", a something "for me." Varela thinks that like this, in a simple and understandable way, with the expression "first person" we are referring to the "conscious experience" or simply to the "experience". This is identical to what Husserl designated "psychical experience"—that is, what in nature possesses the character of an *I*, the experience that in language we call "the first grammatical person", since it provides a point of reference to the second and third grammatical persons. Husserl understands the "I" as everything that inseparably belongs to each living consciousness (as experiencing, thinking, feeling, wanting). Varela, finally, could not help but arrive at practically the same, as, definitely, for him the first person is what appears as relevant and evident for a *self* or *subject,* who can provide a description, given that said experiences, as such, have their "subjective" side. We will return to the meaning of self in this context. The reader surely concurs that subject, conscience, subjective, first person, I, self, ego, experience, etc., is a chain of synonymies. Evidently, one can try to affirm (somewhat brutally in my opinion) that each one of those words expresses a different thing, but to enter into that discussion would result in something perfectly artificial, and it is not the objective of this work. The problem, as we have already repeated, is to establish what kind of relationship exists between these phenomena and what we refer to as "objective"—for example, the physical world or our own body.

The third person

In contrast to the previous, descriptions in the third person (that are paradigmatically the support of scientific research) concern experiences relative to events, such as nature, the planetary system, bacterial reproduction, neurodevelopmental phenomena, or our body as a "biological thing". It is intended that such descriptions are "objective"—that is, *not subjective*—regarding how things truly are, eliminating the distortions that subjectivity supposes. We are not facing a tautology here, but a clear contradiction. If we maintain the idea that there is not "a world itself" waiting to be discovered, then methodologies in third person, simply, could not exist. Yet, on the other hand, can science effectively detach itself from the "subjectivity" (the self) of the researcher? It seems we must answer, *no.* In a strict sense, methodologies in the third person will never be "pure", since they are impossible without the involvement of a "subject". When it is not possible to eliminate the human agents that in science produce and provide descriptions of that "objective" world, the only possible means by which to try to access that world is the belief that the standardised control of the subjective pole, through some form of methodology, keeps it "stably known". However, if from the beginning the inexistence of a *world itself* is stated, the methodological controls, as strict as they are, could not break that initial statement without entering into a clear contradiction, which would force us to start all over again.

The second person

The second person—that is, the singular and plural "you"—is maybe less developed in enactive cognitive science. However, and as we will see later, it is part of the substance of intersubjectivity that, at the same time, supports most human actions and, of course, psychotherapy. The second person is the other "close one", the one who relates to me somehow, the one who establishes a dialogue with me, the one who I care about in a direct way, the one who I love, the one who I admire, the one who matters to me somehow. It is not about "the other in general", as in those people we see on the streets, or those we imagine living in Thailand or Ghana, but another in particular: my wife María Eugenia, or my friend Michele, or my brothers David, Abel, and José Miguel. The second person is a *reciprocity,* since that particular other is related also to me as a particular other for them. In other words, a second person always implies *another* second person. I am a second person to my patients, and they are to me; I am a second person to my daughters, and they are to me. The list includes almost all the important bonds between human beings.

Besides those mentioned, the second person includes a great number of mysteries. It is easier to understand that I am me, or a eucalyptus is a eucalyptus (first and third person, respectively) than to understand the reciprocate link between persons and intersubjectivity. Although our life is absorbed in the second person, that is not an impediment to make it much more difficult to describe it, to develop a knowledge about it and, of course, to explain it.

An epistemological view

It is evident that we are fully within the field of epistemology. Indeed, epistemology comes from the Greek root *episteme,* of which the best-known contemporary meanings are "knowledge" and "science". However, originally its meaning was wider, including notions such as "skill" and "expertise", being part of an ascendant ladder, where reason can access the truth and, beginning with *techne,* passing through *episteme,* ending in *nous.* If we choose "knowing" as the meaning of *logos*, and in that way complete a preliminary idea of what we want to say with "epistemology", then we are entering a maze. Indeed, we are saying we want to know *how* we know or, in other words, we pretend to know how the knowledge is possible. I say "maze", since it is implied that we do know, but also, that we do not know how we get to that knowledge. Evidently, knowledge is not in doubt, only the way to access it. However, who should we ask about the way in which we know? Is that someone different from the one who supposedly knows without any problem? Is that any human being? Let us take on some more detailed considerations. Perhaps the most important—and repeatedly mentioned—of these is the realisation that knowledge, as well as consciousness, is always knowledge *about something.* We know about this and that, but each is necessarily *of* something. That something, from the perspective of a theory of knowledge and for the purpose of being able to communicate—and with all the caution mentioned at the beginning of this book—we can name "the epistemic object". Biology, for example, has living beings as its epistemic object. It knows about them. But, the epistemic object is not simply an individual, as in "this fish", "this mammal" or "that plant". They are individual objects, which are part of biology's field of knowledge, because they share among them, and with other phenomena of nature, an essential community: that of living beings, in the understanding that we are capable of acknowledging life. In this way, the epistemic object of a science is not one or many particular cases, but a class of objects or events that—among many differences—have in common an essential feature, in this case, that of "living" beings. It is because of this that biology must unavoidably ask itself what about a system makes it "life".

A similar thing happens with the one who knows, the one we also in an inappropriate way call "the epistemic subject": it is not about this or that other biologist in particular, but a biologist in general (that is, also as a category) that expresses the requirement of a necessity for somebody or anybody to be a biologist. Both categories—epistemic objects and subject—can be formulated as a relational question: who knows (epistemic subject) about what (epistemic object)?

Who and what. However, on setting out the question, a second one arises between the who and the what: *how* does the biologist know about living beings? That is, how is it possible for the biologist, faced with living beings, to go from minimum knowledge states to major and more rigorous knowledge states? This last question, regarding how, is usually known as methodology.

Method is a derivative form of the Greek *methodos,* meaning also "path" or "way"; a procedure used to get to an end. Strictly, the original meaning points at the road that leads to a place.

Methodology, in many and essential aspects, defines the epistemic feature of the subject and the object. Nobody is a physicist just because of interest, for example, in falling objects, but because of his or her way of going about it. It is not enough for building a science that a subject and a group of objects define some kind of relation; it is necessary also for the relation to be regulated in an explicit, methodological way. Before the method, it concerns individual subjects and objects with no epistemological meaning. We can, then, affirm that epistemology answers an integrated question: "About what and how knows who?" In this conception, what, how, and who are categories and not mere subjects, phenomena or individual styles.

However, it is evident that no person can accomplish anything with this formalisation, since nobody is a category, nor are phenomena categories, although in some cases it is supposed that people adequately trained, and confronted with supposedly equivalent phenomena, should obtain similar results, although this, in general, does not occur. However, in the everyday world, people are not usually restricted in this way. On the contrary, they are always themselves, and not members of an abstract category, which does not imply that these persons lack knowledge. What they lack is an explanation for "how" they get to know.

Pragmatics of experience

Methodologies in the first person aspire to *I* studying myself methodologically, which is why, in a traditional sense, in this situation there would not be another thing except subjectivity, since it entails a subjectivity studying itself as a subjectivity. Is this possible? That is, is it possible for a subjectivity to be on some side an object of that same subjectivity? Can a subjectivity be an object? Maybe. But, maintaining caution, we should continue investigating. What would this be about? It is about trying to experience my experiences, about making them explicit in my consciousness through a procedure and a training that is also explicit. However, does it make sense "to experience the experiences", given that by definition the experiences are nothing else than what has been experienced? Francisco Varela, Pierre Vermersch, and the philosopher Natalie Depraz published a decade ago the book entitled *On Becoming Aware* (Depraz, Varela, & Vermersch, 2003) where they develop in detail first person methods under a subtitle of "a pragmatics of experience". The implicit point here is that it seems we have no consciousness of our being conscious. Or that being conscious implies "degrees" of consciousness of that being conscious. But, have we not said before that consciousness is always a consciousness of "something"? Then, studying consciousness is to study the consciousness of *something*. How could we get to being conscious of a kind of *consciousness "itself"*, *without an object? A consciousness of nothing?* These considerations can be, for the moment, somewhat confusing. Let us, therefore, make an epistemological assumption and say that not all our experiences are *notified* as such. As it is presently understood, the idea of *unconscious experiences* (a contradiction in terms that irritated Sartre) goes around like a bird of prey looking for its kill, which in this case is the type of analysis we are conducting. However, that is another discussion, which for now we can avoid, especially if we still have not developed well enough the road that leads us here. Yet there is a previous and fundamental piece of information that Varela affirms and is self-evident: any method requires skills and learning *incarnated*. One cannot learn how to play tennis theoretically, but rather by playing and ideally being guided in the practice by somebody more advanced in this skill. The conclusion in this case is the premise: skills can be improved with practice. Therefore, the skill to be conscious of this and that, and to be conscious of being conscious, can be trained-in just like any other ability. It would not be daring if somebody stated that, precisely, this is the objective not only of psychoanalytic practice but of any other form of psychotherapy ("to experience my experiences"). Varela and his co-authors harmonise two traditions of "self-knowledge": phenomenology, in the sense developed by Husserl, and Buddhist traditions, especially those based in the practice of *shamatha* ("concentration" or "mindfulness"). We have seen how, in order to devise bridges between the practice of phenomenology and *shamatha*, it is necessary to remember that this concerns, in the first instance, bridges with a methodological character, with independence from their final objectives. However, and in contrast to the epistemology of occidental empirical science (supported in the third person), within these traditions there are no longer the categories of an epistemic subject and object, but of singular persons, of the "every time me" of Heidegger (Rivera, 2001). It is prudent then to ask ourselves: Does phenomenology have a method? Does Buddhist meditation have a method? If yes, then are these methods different, the same, or variations of the same process? Do they arrive at similar conclusions? Is all of this related to psychotherapy? That is what we will try to bring to light in these pages. The task is not simple, since in the case of the aforementioned wisdom traditions, it is necessary to go to direct sources and not to the endless ramifications developed by disciples or supporters. To think, for its part, requires the difficult task of maintaining a logical account and not losing coherence and consistency along some curve of the road. Besides, I should note that reflecting upon phenomenology or Buddhism does not entail an unconditional attachment to these disciplines. As we will see, to be a "phenomenologist" or a "Buddhist", the same as being a Catholic or a Hegelian, is exactly the opposite of what inspires these pages.

CHAPTER TWO

Intentional consciousness

In an article entitled, simply, "Phenomenology", which appeared in the *Encyclopædia Britannica* in 1925 (Husserl, 1998), Husserl helps us by offering some first steps in this matter. "The term 'phenomeno-logy' designates [...] a new kind of descriptive method which made a breakthrough in philosophy at the turn of the century, and an *a priori* science derived from it; a science which is intended to supply the basic instrument (*Organon*) for a rigorously scientific philosophy and, in its consequent application, to make possible a methodological reform of all the sciences" (Husserl, 1998, p. 35). A cryptic sentence. However, we want to emphasise that Husserl probably foresaw, in expressing his proposal in this way, that almost nobody would make sense of it. Therefore, he retraces this statement and suggests that phenomenology requires an access route as a propaedeutic introduction: this route is "phenomenological psychology". In this return *(anabasis)* it is impossible to avoid the question of what the psychic thing is. Husserl answers that it is, "what in nature is found with the *I* character, with all that inseparably belongs to it as to psychic living (as experiencing, thinking, feeling, wanting)" (Husserl, 1998, p. 36). That is, what we find in the universe with the character of "qualia". However, Husserl asks himself if a pure psychology is possible (meaning, in this context, independent of individual subjects and objects), separate from, but in an authentic parallel to the purely physical science of nature (i.e., a kinetic theory, which can be applied equally to apples, rocks and bicycles). As we have seen, one cannot begin with those categories mentioned in the introduction (the epistemic subject and object), but it is necessary to get to them beginning from the experiences in the first person, even though these general laws are put in the very first place of "a priori" (before and first regarding experience). To fulfil this guiding idea, Husserl needs, in the first place, to investigate whether the psychic experience has some peculiarity that can be transformed into a subject of a pure psychology—that is (paradoxically), to transform it into an experience of nobody in particular and of everybody in general. It is obvious that the pre-eminent and immediate psychic experience is, in each case, our own psychism. That is the starting point. Yet, to look to our own psychism there will be a splitting that makes the viewpoint of our consciousness, which was once directed to the world's objects, subsequently turn inwards towards the recent activity of that same consciousness. That is to say, a "flexion" that places the recent activity of consciousness, or consciousness recently occurred, not as mere consciousness, but as an object which my current consciousness can address. As Husserl puts it: "Every experience admits a similar reflection" (Husserl, 1998, p. 38).

Let us examine this more closely. In common conditions, we are directed to what confronts us in the world as the things I use, that I regard and somehow I understand; both other human beings and the presences of nature. Yet also I can be directed to the things I think, or what I make present in my imagination, or the feelings I have for this or that person or situation. What appears at the forefront in all these cases is that to which my current consciousness *refers*. It seems that my consciousness can never be in itself, but rather always, as we have stressed, pointed at "something" that is *not* itself. That which is addressed, what my conscience refers to, has, for Husserl, an evident expression in everyday language, in which we say: "to remember *something*", "to think about *something*", "to perceive *something*", "to aspire to *something*" and so on. Consciousness is, then, only when "something" appears "for" it or, to put it another way, when it is directed to some object (perceptual, imaginary, abstract, etc.). This fundamental character of consciousness or of its "being" is described using a term of scholastic origin: *intentionality*. As we have already outlined, the word *intentionality*, from the Latin term *intendo*, means "to tend in one direction, to stretch, to extend". The concept of "extending" might, in fact, be fundamental to what we are trying to express, since it signifies that something englobes "more space than the space it occupied before". This extension of consciousness contains a curious paradox: on one side consciousness is *always* extended, given that it encompasses all objects to which it is directed yet, on the other side, consciousness and the objects to which it is directed are *distinct*. If we fail to recognise this distinction, we are liable to confuse the perceived tree with ourselves (Ojeda, 2003). There cannot be an object without consciousness and vice versa. The paradoxical matter is that, even this being so, the object and consciousness are different things. This extension, in conclusion, is what is known as *transcendence* and it will attract to itself an important part of the efforts of contemporary philosophy, especially that of Heidegger.

Now, if every consciousness is intentional, and the acts by which it is constituted are perceiving, judging, remembering, etc.—that is to say, psychic acts—then those psychic acts would be intentional. However, these acts do not appear when one is engaged in "direct conscious activity" ("natural attitude", as Husserl would describe it): that is, when perceiving, I perceive *what* is perceived and not *the act* of perceiving; when remembering, *what* is remembered and not *the act* of remembering; when judging, *what* is judged and not *the act* of judging. All of that—what is perceived, what is remembered, and what is judged—is the "object" of consciousness, rather than the act of consciousness through which the said object is constituted. What Husserl argues, however, is that something unique happens if consciousness flexes over itself and "extends" instead to *the unit of itself and its primary or original object recently occurring* and then "holds" that set as a new object for this additionally new consciousness (reflective consciousness). What happens then? Some kind of miracle happens, he says: "Through it (reflective consciousness) we apprehend, instead of pure and simple things (*Sachen*) [...] the corresponding subjective experiences in which they get to be 'conscious' to us, in which, in a very wide sense, they 'appear' to us" (Husserl, 1998, p. 38). This appearance of objects in experience (or psychic acts), whatever it is, Husserl calls a "phenomenon". Yet we should be cautious: the phenomenon we are referring to is not something that simply *belongs* to the world, but neither does it belong to consciousness. Given that, just in the intentional experience, it can happen something like an object, it will always, then, be "experienced" and, therefore, the phenomenon that arises between consciousness and object, more than a mere relationship, is a compact unit.

Phenomenological reduction: a possible method for the first person epistemology

It is pertinent to ask ourselves: how do we practise, the above-mentioned reflective consciousness, which gives us access to the *consciousness-object* complex, that is, to the noetic-noematic complex recently occurred? Husserl proposes, to this end, a procedure not exempt from complexity that he calls "phenomenological reduction" or *epoché* (a Greek word, meaning to put in parentheses, to suspend, to leave disregarded). It is evident that the phenomenological reduction Husserl proposes answers the question regarding the realisation of practice and how every question of that nature seeks a *method.* If I ask how I can remove a ring that is stuck on my finger, I answer: "Using soap and pulling slowly". It concerns a way of doing something that leads to a specific result. A method can be taught, learnt and perfected and, at the same time, expressed through the "steps" of a sequence of actions (Husserl, 1986, 1980). In Husserl's phenomenology, these steps are: reflexivity; scientific, cultural and philosophical *epoché*; description and analysis; imaginary variation or eidetic reduction; and transcendental reduction. For the objectives relevant to us in our endeavour, we refer only to the first four of these steps, as the transcendental reduction is strictly of a philosophical character, the objective of which is also strictly philosophical.

Reflexivity

We have already highlighted that acts of consciousness are directed towards the world in their spontaneous form; to that *something* perceived, imagined, thought or loved. The acts of perceiving, imagining, thinking or loving, through which those said somethings (objects) are constituted, remain mute. The principle of reflexivity, as we have already outlined, consists in making those acts, which are directed to the world, objects of a new consciousness called "reflective consciousness", occurring at a "second time". This consciousness denies its natural direction towards the immediate and present world, forcing its direction instead to a new object that is the retained consciousness with its corresponding objects, which normally tends to be elusive.

The scientific, cultural and philosophical epoché

For psychology, psychopathology, and psychotherapy, the so-called "negative moment"—that of the cultural, philosophical and scientific reduction—is very important. It consists in every phenomenological demonstration being made on the basis of an abstention, consistent in leaving disregarded all judgement with respect to the doctrinal content of the philosophies given beforehand, of beliefs, of casual and scientific assumptions, of theories of diverse natures, and making all demonstrations in the frame of that abstention. To abstain or put in parentheses what has been said does not imply that what has been thus enclosed disappears, but merely implies that, in the disciplined, methodological practice, the enclosed remains in suspension and is not used.

That is, it implies momentarily putting in parentheses or suspending all consideration, conception, explanation, or hypothesis with respect to the phenomenon under investigation, so as to access it in the most unprejudiced way possible. The spontaneous (natural) attitude is immersed in evaluations of widely diverse natures, among which we can highlight comprehensive, theoretical, or causal elaborations that disguise and hide the phenomenon itself. In the field of psychopathology, a typical example of this is to understand the primary delusional experience as a distortion of normal phenomena (as delusional *perception* or delusional *inspiration*), or to see it as a *symptom or sign* of a bodily illness, or to try to reduce it to a known and ordinary phenomenon, such as dreaming, or to understand it as a metaphor or analogous to a merely postulated meaning. An extreme example, in this sense, is to consider the delusion as an "erroneous belief", as it is unscrupulously designated in the *Diagnostic and Statistical Manual of Mental Disorders* (2016). It is not clear how one would think of "delusion" as related to concepts such as "belief" or "mistake". We must emphasise that we are using the word "phenomenon" here in the way outlined above. The "phenomenon" is not about "objects", "things", "persons", etc., but, rather, the consciousness-object complex. In every case, the delusional phenomenon is distorted and blurred *behind* these considerations and cannot, on this account, provide its own phenomenal structure. Given the presence, or merely a vague intuition of delusional experience, these prejudices make the phenomenon itself disappear. The positive moment gives us the phenomenon itself, allowing it to appear before consciousness in a non-contaminated manner.

The practice of the first and second principle of epoché

Does it seem simple? Is it enough for one to understand what we have just mentioned to execute this first methodological step, composed of the two addressed principles (reflexivity and philosophical, scientific and cultural reduction)? This question can also be expressed another way: can we learn to "make" reflection and cultural, scientific and philosophical abstention? Can it be taught? If we suppose that access to consciousness and its objects requires, in the first place, these principles, how can we leave aside these practical and didactical questions? I think the failure of the phenomenological psychopathology programme is related, not only to the shift of the reflexive object from "my consciousness and its objects" to "the other's consciousness and its objects"—that is, to the unexplained methodological change from the first to the second person (that then will be transformed in cognitive sciences into "heterophenomenology", which we should analyse carefully)—but, especially, to the absence of practical, coherent proposals to achieve the exercise of reflection and "abstention", coupled with an abstruse and somewhat tacky language that expels the reader before passing over the threshold. There is no phenomenological text that refers in a systematic way to the practice of the method. Husserl refers to the "what", but not to the "how". In some cases, the practice is simply despised, as in the case of Max Scheler (1958). For him, the phenomenological method is subsequent to prolonged work regarding the things themselves; that is, the method to obtain access to phenomena is subsequent to phenomena themselves, for which it is not clear in what sense a method is necessary.

The ego

What is it to be left disregarded when we say we must abstain from all that has been said a moment ago? What structure embraces our convictions regarding beliefs, our scientific and philosophical ideas, our point of view, our cultural and religious influences and our ethical, aesthetic, social and biographical valuations? It becomes evident that what is common among these influences is that they are to do with me. They are *my* beliefs, *my* valuations, *my* convictions, *my* personal history. It is totally evident that a biologist is a person with a proper name and an unrepeatable biography, with beliefs and convictions, etc. However, one is not a biologist because one's name is Maria or Juan, because one is an only child or because one believes in democracy and gender equality. All of these latter features are parts of our identity *as ego,* which is always the historical, cultural and biographical netting that makes sense of us as persons, and that includes the possibility of us being constituted in this or that way as individuals and as a collective. It is there, in those historical and spontaneous nettings, that the ego constitutes the place in which people create some kind of bonding. The phenomenological attitude is not about me no longer being César or admiring the writer Zadie Smith or having studied philosophy or being a psychiatrist. It is just that, in the phenomenological act, all that constitutes my ego should remain *momentarily* suspended. If I do not achieve sufficient abstention, the world, other people, and everything that is *not-me* will be apprehended with a bias and a tonality filtered by my ego and, thereby, will be to a greater or lesser extent self-referential.

Nothing of what has been said is addressed explicitly by phenomenology. However, in conceiving, as Husserl does (and as Varela repeats), that consciousness is that in the universe which has the character of "I", "ego" or "self" and that the phenomenological method must begin from there, the matter becomes more arduous, because it is assumed *that consciousness is the ego.*

Consciousness, "subjectivity" and the ego

Is it not the "first person" that we want to access through *epoché,* the ego as identity (my "I")? Is the ego not constituted by the knot of every system of beliefs, theories and conceptions of the world and experiences that each person has, that is, the biography knitted with these threads, and that this is precisely what we want to leave in parentheses? Maybe the answer to these questions lies in the fact that studying consciousness *does not seem the same* as studying the ego. Jean Paul Sartre, interested in Husserl and staying in Germany at the time, wrote *The Transcendence of the Ego* in 1934 (Sartre, 1988). His reflection is keen and counter-intuitive, but at the same time, amazing. He holds that consciousness *does not have inhabitants:* no object (in a wide sense, including things, persons, ideas, and fantasies, etc.) is "inside" consciousness. On the contrary, consciousness is "directed to them", or they "appear" to consciousness, but they are not "in" consciousness. It is for this reason that objects are not immanent, but rather transcendent. Transcendent in philosophical language does not necessarily mean "important", or of greater value or duration. It means, in its most immediate sense (of *trans*, "beyond", and *scando*, "scaling") to pass from one area to another, surpassing the limit that separates the two. Fundamentally, then, what we are saying is that objects are not "inside" of consciousness (immanent) but beyond it and, thus, "outside" (transcendent). This is evident in the case of perception: if I perceive a tree, it is not inside my consciousness and neither is it a replica or a "simulacrum" (Sartre liked this word). In the cases of thinking, imagining, remembering and feeling, the matter is perhaps somewhat more counter-intuitive, yet it has the same structure. Sartre developed this last issue some years later in *The Imaginary* (Sartre, 1964). One can *reach* objects with different kinds of consciousness, in the way that I can perceive, imagine or remember *the same object*, in this case, the tree. Imagining, remembering or thinking are not *inside* consciousness either, but they are *modes* of consciousness and every mode is *that kind* of consciousness alone. From "beginning to end" consciousness reaches the object intentionally, but in a determinate mode and not in any mode.

We will delve into this point later on. For now, it is enough to say that, if we follow the outlined reason, it is the ego that should be put in parentheses in this first methodological stage, as this is all we wish to disregard at this point. We will use the words "ego", "self" and "I" equivalently, understanding that there are diverse conceptions of each, but that such distinctions are not the concern of this essay. In the phenomenological attitude, the suspension of the ego is not a value judgment, it is merely a methodological step. If we could achieve that cultural, scientific abstention and all else mentioned above, if we could put the ego in parentheses, as a result *we would not find anything like unconsciousness*. We are not talking about an exceptional experience—frequently and daily our consciousness is free of ego. Concentrating on something is enough to achieve this state. If you are repairing an old watch and trying to understand its gears, its operation, and looking for what is preventing its functioning, you, as ego, disappear. If we are in a psychotherapy session, the more intense moments are those in which the therapist disappears as himself, as identity, as ego. If we are absorbed in a thought, an image, a lecture or a movie and the phone rings, we experience a breakdown that brings us back to our identity, age, biography and condition. But, in all these cases, we were nevertheless perfectly conscious. Your ego is present in psychotherapy if you are not with the patient, but worried about your fees. Or in your job as a watchmaker and not in the watch you have in front of you. Or if you include in the reading of a novel the view of the literary technics, for example, regarding a work you are writing. For Sartre, the ego is *always the object* of consciousness and never consciousness itself. It is from this point that his book derives its title. This insight is extraordinarily relevant, given that Sartre adds something crucial for common sense: *consciousness is impersonal*, since identity is in the ego, and the ego is an object of consciousness and never consciousness itself.

The description

If we succeed in this step, the consciousness-object complex emerges in a wide sense, by which our consciousness is referred to as the phenomenon. But this is not enough. Now it is necessary (from an epistemological perspective) to describe this consciousness with no self-reference. How do we learn to describe our own states of consciousness (those that we have discussed thus far)? Let us attempt a phenomenological description with an example. I am imagining my daughter on her way over for lunch. It is evident that she is not in front of me perceptually but, without a doubt, she is in front of my consciousness *now*. If I try, at the same time, to look at the lamp that is in front of me, I stop imagining, or I experience a kind of oscillation. Or I focus on the perceived lamp, or on the imagined face of my daughter, but I cannot hold both states simultaneously. I realise that, when imagining, the image (or *imago*) has a kind of blurriness, making it difficult to analyse. It is not related to anything that is perceptually in front of me. It is not proximate, as is the desk or the top of the shelf. Besides, my wife, who just arrived in the office, also sees the lamp from another angle, and the same occurs to me if I move around the lamp or any other object of perception, but my wife cannot access from another angle my daughter's face in my imagination. Further, I can be wrong about the nature of what is perceived: I might think there is a spider on the wall, but move closer and confirm it is a stain. We say, then, that in perception illusion is possible. Yet, nobody can convince me that, when imagining my daughter's face, I am in fact imagining somebody that is similar to her. We could continue, and extensively.

What have we done? In this first attempt, we have properly described neither the lamp nor my daughter's face. Therefore, we have not described the objects of my consciousness, but rather *the way of being an object in two different modes of consciousness. We have not described consciousness as if it were an object, but just two ways in which objects are present to it.* We could go further in this example, or in any other, as remembering, fantasizing, understanding, and abstracting, acting, etc.

The eidetic reduction

Let us suppose that we have described two modes of consciousness: the imagining and perceptual consciousness. What matters is that it is possible to do so independently of the specific example object. It might be my daughter's imagined face and the perception of a lamp, or the image of my friend Marco and the perception of a lizard lying in the sun in the front yard. This is possible because we have practised the "reflection", the first methodological principle. We are not describing just objects, but phenomena or, to put it another way, the shapes in which the objects appear to my consciousness. As we have already noted, a single object can appear to one's consciousness in diverse forms.

The eidetic reduction, as with every *epoché*, requires that we disregard some aspects. What must be disregarded in this case? To describe the imagining consciousness, *it is not necessary* for it to be my daughter's face. It can be any object and, whichever I imagine, all will have the same general features described. I can, then, put my daughter's face in the parentheses. What is clear is that, independent of what the object is, there must be an object. The same is true of other modes of consciousness: I can perceive a painting or the sea I view from my window. All that is perceived in particular will present to me in a determinate form of consciousness, perceptual consciousness, and those perceived objects—such as, for example, a lamp, a painting or the sea—having served as material for this process, can be suspended, or reduced. Again, it is clear that, despite the difference of consciousness from the object itself, there must be *some* object. What is surprising is that, if I stop for a moment in any state of consciousness, I discover that I can distinguish it from others without difficulty: I do not confuse the perceived with the imagined or the remembered with the understood. Having now obtained the general description of every state of consciousness, I can ask myself another question: of the described, what aspect *cannot* be eliminated without undoing that mode of consciousness for my reflective consciousness? Could a perceptual consciousness build its object "just for me" as does the imagining consciousness? If it did, the object would not be constituted to us as perception. Could I corporeally pounce upon the given object constituted in the imagining consciousness? Evidently, no. I can continue like this in a differentiating process until I discover which features are necessary for the constitution of each kind of consciousness.

This being clear, I can also focus on the *objects* of this consciousness that I reach through reflection. If I perceive, imagine, or remember my daughter, I can ask myself what affords me certainty that it is her. I can imagine or perceive or remember many very different persons. What, then, is the essential aspect of my daughter reached by any of these modes of consciousness? We will not answer this question here, as it would take us many pages, but what we can affirm is that my daughter would not be herself if she had Michele's features. We can say, then, that there are *certain features* necessary for a person to be what he or she is to my consciousness, without which, or replaced by others, they would vanish as that specific person. We anticipate here that retention (that is, memory and protention, or anticipation) is fundamental. The exercise of varying the features of objects given to my consciousness is called eidetic variation, and it not only permits us to find the essential features of the different modes of consciousness, but also the essential features of any object given by these modes.

At this point, something of great practical importance has happened: once the essential features of consciousness or an object are described through reflection, *we find that we are no longer in a field of facts*. The same is the case if the imagining consciousness is directed to my daughter's face, or a landscape of black trees, or one particular dog or another. We have arrived at what Husserl called the *eidos* or "essence" of an object of consciousness, but we have done so by known steps and with explicit evidence. It is from this idea that we derive the term "eidetic (i.e., essential) reduction". This jump from facts to essences is a jump of field, as we can now acknowledge the way in which perception, imagination or emotion presents to us anytime, anywhere and in anybody, and we can also recognise the essential features of any object, without which that object would no longer be an object of a specific kind. The problem is no longer empirical (or, with more reason, statistical). As Husserl noted, the three lengths of a triangle cut in a point independently of when and where Aristotle, you, or I think. If we maintain some kind of scepticism regarding the utility of this exercise, we can ask ourselves: what kind of consciousness and what kind of objects constitute delusion or hallucination or melancholy or obsessive-compulsive disorder or phobia? To answer this question we must realise that, as clinicians and not philosophers, we are not merely discussing *our consciousnesses* and their objects, but also those of patients. Nevertheless, we must establish that the patients are not and *should not be* focussed on a phenomenological attitude. This means that their ego is not suspended. On the contrary, their ego is a fundamental, relevant, and essential part of their subjectivity.

Heterophenomenology

Daniel Dennett titles Chapter Four of his five hundred-page bestseller, *Consciousness Explained* (Dennett, 1991), "A Method for Phenomenology". The surprising thing is that, in the extensive bibliography of the book, there is not one mention of Edmund Husserl and, in that chapter, not one reference to phenomenology as such. I mention this because Dennett's abundant statements do not inspire me enough to expend the effort to dismantle his enormous castle of naïve empiricism. Let us just say that, for him, phenomenology is Descartes' position and his first person is reflected in *cogito ergo sum*. This radical ignorance does not offer even a pretence at explaining consciousness, and saves us any need to penetrate the *sauté* his book presents. However, the term he coins, "heterophenomenology", seems like it could be useful if placed in an appropriate context—that is, one that attempts to do phenomenology without skipping, precisely, phenomenology itself. The consciousness we have studied thus far has been "mine" (self-phenomenology). But, as we addressed earlier, we—psychiatrists, psychotherapists, psychopathologists and clinical psychologists—have as a reference the subjectivity of an "another", and his or her experiences are those that we wish to understand, analyse, and know in their essential aspects. Evidently heterophenomenology, contrary to what Dennett would prefer, is not about experimental subjects in a laboratory following instructions and pressing buttons, nor about transcriptions of verbal language, or videos with the goal of transforming their subjectivity into "data" that allow for their inclusion in the mechanisms of empirical science. The question of whether phenomena in the first person can be moved by means of checklists and scales to the third person and transformed into objects for "science" cannot be eluded. If this question is not answered thoroughly, we will find ourselves with merely an illusion of "scientificity". Is it possible to study subjectivity by pulling it out of subjectivity, that is, to study it from outside itself?

We have already mentioned Varela's insuperable contradiction between phenomenology and his biological constructivism, which postulates that there is not a world itself, "out" there, liable to be reached by a biological system (conscious, in this case). Under this constructivism, there is no possibility of transcendence nor intentionality (reaching objects, including ego), in the sense mentioned above. But it is evident that science, as we have noted, pretends to study an "objective" world that is out there, and that this world is investigated by "subjects" who interpret their "data" through "conventions", assuming that conventions are a guarantee of knowledge of a "superior and independent level" and that data can replace experienced phenomena. From there comes Varela's futile efforts to, in our judgment, integrate autopoietic neurobiological data with phenomenology and Buddhism (which we will introduce to our approach at the appropriate time). A small argument from authority pleases us at this point, as it was Sartre who said that those who start from "data" never get to "essences".

However, without becoming entangled in premature argumentation, we can affirm that in heterophenomenology one tries to access the subjectivity of another, of a "second person", rather than one's own. Yet it takes only a little advance for us to realise that there are not "second persons" as such. A second person is always relative to a first: there is no you, he, she or it without a founding I (the same occurs for the plural). For every you there is an I, and for every he, she or it, there is an "anchor" I. Without a first person there is no possibility of something "other". In a world of millions of conscious beings, then, heterophenomenology is about a system of relative points that cross one another in a very complex way. Maria, who goes to my office, sees me as a you, as a second person. I see her also as a you and a second person. Neither I nor she can come out of the first person, of being "every time me". As we will see in the chapters relating to psychotherapy, the difference in that context is that the second person is constituted with the ego of the therapist suspended.

Taking the above into account, and returning to our clinical work, we can separate this heterophenomenology into two types. The first refers to another (you) who is looking for personal training as a clinician, with the objective of achieving in himself or herself the "phenomenological attitude". The second type refers to the experience of "another" who is not in the apprentice position, but in the "patient" position, or the person who has requested our professional help.

CHAPTER THREE

Phenomenology

W e have already mentioned that, in the texts of philosophical and psychopathological phenomenology, there is not the slightest reference to a practical method that would allow for the reduction of the "natural attitude" and its transformation into the "phenomenological attitude".

The phenomenology apprentice

Is it possible to teach the phenomenological attitude? Is it possible to learn it and perfect it? We will begin with the concept of the *apprentice*, but with a clear condition that the positions of "master" and "apprentice" do not permit any hierarchical connotations, that is, any connotations of supremacy, power, or authority. It merely concerns stages related to lived time and practice. The master is not necessarily "better" or possessed of greater "capacities" than the apprentice. All hierarchical positions be disregarded here, in this way forming the essential basis of everything we have said.

What does the apprentice of phenomenology need? In the field of their own "psyche" or "mind", he or she must perform the steps of reflection, scientific and cultural abstention, or *epoché*, and imaginary variation, at least. If this is not accomplished, it is very difficult for the apprentice truly to see the presentation to their clinical consciousness of another (i.e., the patient) as that "other" alone and not contaminated with the apprentice's own ego, which is not sufficiently inactivated. We must clarify that it is not about living always in a phenomenological attitude, but being able to activate it in the clinical situations that merit it. It is evident, after all, that we cannot ignore the self. The phenomenological attitude is an ability acquired, like playing tennis, but nobody will suppose that in daily life one thus trained should be always playing tennis. Since phenomenology is not an ordinary practice (we live normally in the natural attitude), it is necessary to start with theoretical knowledge that first allows the apprentice to understand the phenomenological attitude, at least conceptually. This first step is full of difficulties, as phenomenological writings use language in a special way and are very heterogeneous. However, an adequate selection and a consistent guide will allow the apprentice to gain understanding, slowly and meticulously. Nothing is complex if the corresponding language is mastered.

What are the first practical exercises? Given the absolute lack of methodological practice in philosophical phenomenology, we think it is necessary that we orient ourselves to Buddhist practice. To those who consider that introducing traditions of knowledge external to our occidental world is a form of esotericism, we ask for patience. As mentioned in the introduction, what phenomenology and Buddhism have in common is the *methodological search* that tends to produce states of impersonal consciousness, understanding that every method is a way of doing, that is, a practice (*praxis*), though this not been clearly expressed in phenomenology. Buddhist meditation is a road that allows for the completion of the necessary steps to achieve a state in which consciousness *is free from self*. This is possible on the condition that one does not confuse the ego with consciousness. As we have highlighted, ego is never consciousness itself but rather an "object of consciousness", as is the tree I perceive from the window of my desk.

Meditation practice

There are many forms and variations of meditation within different Buddhist schools. The form conceived and practised by Chögyam Trungpa, presented in his book *Shambhala* (Trungpa, 1986), seems to us especially suited to our purposes in its initial steps and fundamental principles. It can be initiated by sitting on the ground or on a cushion that is not too high, and crossing one's legs in the tailor's position. This generates a stable physical state with a good support base, remembering that our body is subject to the same gravitational laws as other living or inert bodies. It can also be performed sitting in a chair with both legs parallel and supporting the soles of the feet on the ground. The vertebral column must be straight, as stooping prevents ideal breathing and affects the axis of corporeal balance. The spine can be pleasantly stretched more than five centimetres. The pelvis must move forward, up to its natural limit. Shoulders should be loose and dropped, spontaneously and without force, and the head should be straight. The eyes can stay open, resting on a more or less fixed point a few meters away, or they can be shut. Attention must then be directed to diaphragmatic breathing (that is, to the abdomen, which moves to generate the entrance and exit of air) and the air passing through the nostrils. The inhalation and exhalation must be soft and, initially, timed to a count of four with a small interval between each. It is about finding a pleasant and precise rhythm for each person (like jogging, after long practice).

Initially, this exercise must be practised daily for at least fifteen minutes. At first, many interferences will challenge the attempt: it is to be expected that the fifteen minutes will feel very long and that consciousness will be invaded by thoughts, feelings, memories, corporeal sensations, fantasies, sounds, etc., distracting us from the breathing on which we wish to focus.

As we repeatedly bring awareness back to our breathing and its full presence (breathing is the most evidently "now" act within our experience), those interferences will diminish. When they occur, they will appear evidently as an interruption, and the return of the consciousness to the breathing, although difficult at first, once achieved demonstrates that detaching from such interference is perfectly possible. As the process advances, we become aware each time of being more in the present centre of our existence, and of this centre being "impersonal" because it lacks history and self-reference. In this way, we can say that we achieve a methodological "forgetting" of our biographical identity. In other words, we are achieving, through this simple exercise, the placing within parentheses or leaving disregarded that which constitutes our self. However, as simple as the exercise appears—its regular, systematic, and progressive practice—it is tough. With time we prove that our body is not something that floats in an imaginary space, but is in fact heavy, and its weight is supported by a chair, a sofa, a cushion, or whatever. In turn, what supports us is ultimately the Earth. There is no metaphor in this: I mean literally the planet. To feel it, to leave it be and take account of it, is a full present moment that allows us the direct experience of being part of a huge totality. Normally we feel that our existence is supported as a self-contained unit (monadic), which is experienced in the cranial, thoracic, and abdominal cavities: in these we feel anguish, sorrow, pleasure, and our conscious being. Given that they are cavities, they offer the impression of an "internal space". The vertebral column, the coccyx area, the ischium and the limbs seem to be merely appendices or "infrastructure". Have you ever thought of your legs as having an "internal" world? As we have mentioned, in the basic technique of meditation the body can hold itself with greater and greater authority on its fundamental support. This point of support is very powerful, because it is nothing less than the ground of our entire existence. That is why earthquakes are so distressing, when all that is solid is suddenly unstable, and at the same time immense power is expressed. Our existence is no longer supported by cavities, but rather by solid parts concordant with gravity. So to speak, our existence is very well-supported, and this fact holds great importance with regard to receiving what the other (in this case, the patient) says, and the way in which he or she says it, without losing our balance. It aids us in maintaining a clear awareness that he or she is a part, also, of that whole. Further, to receive disqualifying verbal aggression is not the same experience when we are breathing with the thorax and supported by a high point of our body, unstable due to its floating position and its distance from the fundamental point of support, as opposed to the same from a serene and firm rooting, with the centre of gravity supported in the natural corporeal triangle. Caroline Brazier (2003) makes a comparison with parabolic aerials that search for signals in outer space: they must be grounded in a large and solid supporting base so as not to cloud the signals received with irregularities or instabilities in their own structure. In this way, the surface of the reception plate remains clean.

The surprising thing in the therapeutic situation is that this solidity is not a psychological power or a personality structure or an "internal" process of the therapist, that is, it is not a mental state achieved and stable. It is, rather, a fundamentally physical, concrete state. Nevertheless, it is difficult to obtain. To forget this aspect of our existence allows us to believe that a self-sufficient spirituality, without a body, disembodied and floating in a heaven of beliefs, is possible. This belief is, as are all beliefs, invisible to our awareness, hidden by the ego, along with personal and cosmological stories. In beliefs we live, said José Ortega y Gasset. There is no doubt that the body has been abused and, not rarely, despised by the occidental culture in which we live, although the contrary is seen at the superficial level. Ultimately, however, there is a tendency to disfigure the body, to cover it, to abuse it, and, fundamentally, to deny it. Phenomena such as grooming, make-up, dressing, and disfiguring rituals (including today's brutal "cosmetic" surgeries) are perhaps a direct expression of this approach to the body and, as we will see, of the unavoidable tension between our project of ourselves and the autonomous script, pre-eminent and unstoppable, of our body as dynamic nature. If we do not acknowledge that nature is also a part of what we are, if we do not acknowledge the totality of what constitutes us and where we belong, the tension, the conflict, and the suffering may be crushing.

The above-described procedure, to the extent possible, must be guided and taught by another who is advanced in the exercise, since to understand and discuss it, as with any other skill, aids in its perfection.

Consciousness of "the otherness"

In this first step, the apprentice is concerned with his or her own "subjectivity" and not with the other's. However, once the present state of consciousness free of ego (or full consciousness) is achieved, it is possible to open up to "the other" in a new way. It is about the "other" visiting us just the way they are and not laden with our needs. However, the otherness is not just the perception of the other and of what is happening in the environment at this moment, but also of different psychic states that visit us. In contrast to when we were practising meditation and rejected these various psychic states, we can now permit them, feel them, and see them in their own composition. We can focus, in this stage, on what we perceive and what we remember, on the emotions we have, on the fantasies that reach us when we are before the other. The first thing to note is that such states are not exactly a full consciousness of myself (the ego). We can, therefore, open up to those modes by which consciousness reaches its objects and discover in these modes things never thought before. To focus reflexively on perception, imagination, memory, feeling, experience, etc., is now full of amazing teachings: a thought comes, then a memory, then an emotion, then my body, which touches my awareness. We also find that our experience is extremely quick and varied: suddenly I perceive, then I feel, then I imagine, then I remember, in a vertiginous and uncontrollable chain, and the script of that sequence is not organised by "me" (the ego). The most surprising thing is that these are sequential states, which are not mixed. They *run*, as does verbal speech, that is, different intentional states (like letters or words) link together in a chain and conform to a syntax, precisely because they are different. The same with the same cannot be articulated. In this way, we also find that, as quick as the process is, we can distinguish, without confusing a fantasy with a perception or with a memory. The fact that the memory could be of this or that is far from irrelevant at this stage. What is irrelevant is my belief that I own such memory, my belief that, due to the fact of having once experienced the event remembered, it belongs to me, it is "mine", and I maintain dominance over it. Memory, like all other experience, simply reaches us.

The second person in the therapeutic field

The phenomenological attitude, acquired in this way, starts with my subjectivity but can then be referred to by other person(s). The same way in which my consciousness, through reflection, is directed to multiple states of consciousness and their objects (imaginary, perceptual, or remembered) and having acknowledged that there are different ways of reaching objects, the next step is now to address another who is also an "object" of our consciousness and who is somehow reached while appearing as another. This does not imply that the other is a "thing", as the word "object" suggests. The matter is more complex, but to treat of it at the moment would divert us severely from the purpose of this reflection. We simply want to note that the other is exactly that: something not-me, different from a rock but not in the sense relevant for this "otherness". Yet the clinician does not find himself or herself before just any person—not before one who merely passes by my side on the street, nor one who is close to me and a determinant of my biographical *locus*—but rather before a person in the position of having requested help. It is usual to believe that a human being is so complex (compared to the perception of a tree, for example), that a long process is required before one can know him or her. Yet this belief arises from a prejudice and not from experience: we know much about the other upon first contact, which does not mean that we have all the stories of him or herself. If we are serene and in a phenomenological attitude, however, the other will present to us with a *certain* simplicity. This means that their attitude, their appearance, the structure of their speech, and their way of treating us, renders evident at first sight their emotional and affective disposition. This does not mean we can explain the processes that are in effect—no matter how much information we have about the other, let us remember that those explanations have been left now in parentheses or disregarded. Therefore, phenomenological descriptions refer fundamentally to these aspects of the encounter that leave *suspicion* aside, that leave aside the idea that what the other presents to us is not what he or she is, but a superficial expression of the real thing that remains hidden. This is not to deny the hidden and the invisible in the psychic life of human beings. It is rather about reflecting on the nature of that invisibility. This reflection will keep us occupied in a subsequent chapter.

CHAPTER FOUR

Psychotherapy

We who practise psychotherapy professionally are not few and we perform that role daily and with many people. Nevertheless, I frequently do not acknowledge my profession as a psychotherapist in many of the innumerable writings and studies that refer to it. Possibly this is also the case for some of those reading these words. It seems to me that, in a certain way, the psychotherapist is *closed down* in his or her profession. Neither the "patient" nor the psychotherapist can be witnesses nor express adequately the process in which they both find themselves. The idea that the psychotherapist can be an "emotionally responsive witness" is no more than an oxymoron, coined seemingly inadvertently by Donna Orange (2013). The witness observes, does not interfere, does not participate, is merely a chance component in the system; he or she was simply passing by and the accident, the murder, or the robbery occurred. It is obvious that that is what it means to be outside. Yet we therapists are, in a certain way, inside, we are part of the process we observe. If neither the therapist nor the patient are witnesses, the therapy landscape is a show without an audience, a sunset that nobody can watch, the world before the appearance of the first human being on the planet (Chardin, 1967), a language not destined for an audience or an external reader. The idea of the ability to be "in and out", in a technical oscillation, is a postulate very difficult to demonstrate. Perhaps that idea is just a natural reaction to avoid the sometimes painful primary, closed, and complex intimacy in which psychotherapy consists. Yet some have also intended to understand the psychotherapeutic process not as an oscillation, but as an observation radically "outside", precisely from the position of the witness. There are expert investigators in psychotherapy who do not practise it, who look rather from the stalls and then analyse, measure, and comment on the "staging". It is similar to what art critics do. "Critique" means, ultimately, a dissection of the piece under review, a separation of its ingredients, an analysis (let us remember that *lisis* is disaggregation). Like every analysis, such a critique is unable to capture synthesis: it only sees parts, pieces, foreshortening. Put brutally, the perspective in the third person, which we have described above, is treated as though it were external and thus, in that belief and given the epistemological value this belief is attributed, can severely disfigure what it aims to understand. In therapy, synthesis is something like a landscape, and the landscape and its performance do not have parts: in twilight everything is twilight. It is not a composition like an assembled puzzle. It is not the reddish horizon, plus the slowed-down waves, plus the somewhat warm breeze. Twilight is just when there is somebody "inside". This is not naïve constructivism. I am not the creator of the sun, the luminosity, the breeze, the warmth or my own existence. No. Twilight is created with me (or with anybody) "inside". While the therapist facilitates, he or she does not create therapy as therapy: he or she is in it as consciousness. The patient "configures" the psychotherapist and the psychotherapist "configures" the patient (the same way the artist "creates" the art work and the art work "creates" the artist, as Heidegger put it, or consciousness "creates" the object and the object "creates" consciousness). The configuration, of which each is a part, is not the property of the psychotherapist or the patient, but rather appears in a kind of "between", of an *interesse,* with particular features that we will examine in due course. From this expression in Latin comes the term "*interés*" in Spanish and "interest" in English. Perhaps it is from here that all story, analysis, or estrangement of the psychotherapeutic process suffers a deformation that is well-intended, but unavoidable. It is possible that each one of us, made to create such a story, assembles, writes out, and describes our psychotherapeutic work without accounting for it correctly. The empirical studies (in the third person) that evaluate the efficacy of psychotherapy tend to discover, after much "data" analysis, that it is the "therapeutic bond" that, to a large extent, makes psychotherapeutic work effective. This is the equivalent of saying that psychotherapy is effective due to psychotherapy itself (which is not an oxymoron, but a tautology that might be called in Spanish "a paradox of Perogrullo"; or, in English, "a statement of the bleeding obvious"). Witnesses—that is, external observers—in their efforts at finding something "objective", must simplify the discipline to the extent that the heart of the matter slips out between their fingers. Maybe we should ask ourselves if each one of us "doing" psychotherapy would do it in the same way with somebody looking through the keyhole. The main obstacle here is that an external observer impedes the psychotherapist's maintenance of a phenomenological attitude, as his or her ego (not his or her conscious-ness) tends to reappear under the observation of a third party. This is analogous to what happens if the therapist is not adequately trained and, thus, what he or she "knows" becomes an obstacle between his or her pure consciousness and the "other".

To achieve psychotherapeutic intimacy before the gaze of a third party is very difficult and not rarely obscene (in the sense of putting on a stage what usually occurs, in essence, without any sense of per-formance). That is why shyness and embarrassment arise always under external and strange observation. Shyness appears as a very powerful barrier that protects the intimate, hiding and disguising it before the eyes of "third persons". It is unnecessary to analyse this here, but it is relevant to mention that public language has a very different structure from intimate language. Additionally, from these considerations it is understandable that, in the case of psychotherapy, it is easier to notice the "external" aspects of the process (the only possibility for a third person).

The external view

Psychotherapy is a way of praxis, it is something that is carried through, that is, it is a way of coping with what confronts us, as are the things I use and handle: my computer, the coffee maker or my shoes. The dif-ference is based on the fact that the psychotherapist must cope with persons and, therefore, the encounter settles from the beginning into a fundamental symmetry (the "asymmetry" usually discussed by psy-chotherapy texts is not ontological, but of power) as the beings that are encountered are of the same kind. Heidegger reserved the word "application" (*Füsorge*) to refer to our treatment of other persons and differentiated it from "care" (*Sorge*), which is our treatment of the beings of the world, that is, of "things" (Heidegger, 1997). Yet this is so general as to include all possible treatments between people, which is why it is necessary to go further and specify. Apart from the mentioned symmetry, what kind of encounter is the psychotherapeutic encounter? Of course, it is a paid, agreed encounter and has, in general, a fixed time, or "session". To put this characterisation in negative terms, it is not about a free, spontaneous, and open encounter, as all human relationships once were, including various forms that would fit, without doubt, into the idea of a helping relationship. But, fundamentally, psychotherapy is a *commercial* encounter, given that somebody pays another for something that, it is supposed, he or she has to offer and that the other person needs. Further, psychotherapy is a contractual encounter, as it establishes itself on rules of exchange, distinct from spontaneous relations—that in general are public social rules that prevail in a culture—and it is a contextually controlled encounter because it establishes a precise frame for such exchange. Additionally, psychotherapy demands an intimate attitude with no previous history: what is given and what is received is not the natural product of an interpersonal history that enters the field of intimacy in a spontaneous way.

If psychotherapy is as described here, it is obvious that, as in any contractual human relationship, psychotherapy requires what legally is called "ability", that is, the contracting parties have the appropriate aptitude, which, in this case, consists of the ability to understand what is agreed and the liberty to accept or decline the terms.

The other (the patient)

As we start there are already difficulties, and they are not minor. Does the patient understand what—so to speak—he or she is implicitly "signing" in the psychotherapeutic contract? In most cases the spontaneous patient (that is, not the candidate psychotherapist) does not have the knowledge and experience to know exactly what he or she is entering into, and neither is it simple to explain. What happens if we take some of Lacan's ideas seriously—and effectively, if that is how they should be taken—and we say to the patient that we do not have anything to give and that they do not know what they are lacking? (Lacan, 2003). Or that we are not there for their "welfare", but for them to love, since what they are lacking they will acquire as a lover? We must add, of course, that in this context love is a metaphoric substitution between the loved and the lover and that it is based in a discordance, given that the lover (in this case, the patient) does not know what they are lacking and the loved (in this case, the therapist) does not know what he or she has. Love, including transference love, is, for Lacan, always trapped in this discordance.

I understand this seems an elaborate example. Let us try another, simpler in appearance. We can say to the patient that he or she suffers from a mental "disorder", for example, an anxiety disorder. This said, we inform him or her that, according to the "meta-analysis" the evidence-based studies offer us, such suffering is ameliorated with behavioural therapy, cognitive behavioural therapy, or therapy of dynamic orientation, or with some drugs or placebo and, even better, with combinations of these, and that for many other forms of psychotherapy we simply do not have enough data to affirm or deny their efficacy. We can add, besides, that the result is noticeably better with new therapists than with those who are expert or famous. Of course, it is possible to say that we have made a caricature, and that although the patient does not have the knowledge or experience to know exactly what they are about to engage in, generally what they know is enough and, besides, they trust that the expert does know what is best for him or her. This merely gives rise to a new problem, as, advertently or not, the implication is that the patient is acting on trust. But from where does this trust come? What does the patient know about the therapist? Do they know anything about the therapist's training or personal history, or his or her professional or academic qualifications? Maybe in some cases the patient might know something, but what seems to be the more common case is that this trust gesture is supported by another trust gesture: what some trustworthy person said to the patient about this particular therapist. That is, the psychotherapeutic act, in the main, is initiated based on a chain of trust.

The therapist

While we have more than enough reason to doubt the knowledge that the patient has about the psychotherapeutic process in which they become engaged, it seems that this question would be improper regarding the therapist: we suppose that the therapist does know. But, what does he or she know? Let us repeat what has been said many times before: with relatively wide criteria, we can count over 400 forms of psychotherapy. That means, among other things, that what therapists think we need to know and what they know-to-do in psychotherapeutic praxis, can be very different things.

We can call fitness (aptitude, adaptation) the ability of a psychotherapeutic model (any of those 400 forms) to inspire the adherence of psychotherapists. It is evident that not all psychotherapy models are equally fit, and those that have very many adherents are few. Further, the quantity of adherents follows a downward gradient that tends towards zero. The probability for models, which are ranked below twenty in terms of popularity, to gain new adherents is very low. Usually, this distribution is called the Power Law in network theory. It is possible to use this kind of theory to study the external aspects of psychotherapy, as it concerns nodal systems (psychotherapeutic models) and links (the adherent therapists). Yet what relation exists between the number of adherents of a model and the "truth", that is, the capacity of the model to offer an effective account of what, effectively and essentially, happens in psychotherapy? Let us suppose that therapists' adherence is not related to the truth of the model: then the essential theoretical foundation of the Freudian approach, that is, the "dynamic unconscious", would be, with regards to "truth", more or less at the same level as behavioural and cognitive behavioural models (and others with high adherence) that, precisely, do not consider such a concept to be relevant. To put it more concisely: those psychoanalytic therapies *without* a dynamic unconscious (as truth) should collapse, and cognitive behavioural therapies *with* a dynamic unconscious (as truth) should also collapse. The point is that they do not collapse, but in fact operate perfectly well with incompatible and, in many ways, contradictory "truths". Thus, remaining cautious in the inducement of conclusions, the "truth" of the model does not seem relevant to its fitness. With some explicit judgement of "truth" we could perfectly well conclude that model number 327 is more truthful than model number 2, even though model 327 has just one adherent: its creator.

If "truth" does not play a relevant role in the adherence of therapists to different psychotherapeutic models, then, with what phenomenon are we faced? To try to answer this question we should return briefly to examine the well-known and sometimes over-used results of empirical investigations of recent decades into psychotherapy and two of its more notable paradoxes: the paradox of "equivalence" and, what we have come to call, the paradox of "belief".

Medical model and contextual model

It is widely known that the absolute efficacy of psychotherapy (by comparison to non-treatment) is today solidly documented. The point of this discussion is to uncover the aspect of psychotherapy that explains this result. The many empirical evaluation efforts regarding the relative efficacy of different psychotherapeutic approaches have concluded that there exists in this regard a Dodo effect, also called an "equivalence paradox". That is, these evaluations have concluded that all studied forms of psychotherapy have approximately equal efficacy. In consequence, the conflict between the various psychotherapeutic models has given way to an extension of the conceptual field, where now there is space for two "metamodels" known, respectively, as the "medical model" and the "contextual model". These metamodels cut the specific models transversely, so to speak.

The medical model postulates that psychotherapy is effective because it involves specific, technical ingredients consistent with the theory, which act selectively on specific psychopathological aspects, in the same way that metformin acts specifically on, for example, the insulin receptors in patients with type 2 diabetes. This model's prediction is that the adherence of therapists to these technical specifications has, as a consequence, better treatment efficacy as compared to non-adherence, in the same way that administering sensitizers to insulin receptors has greater efficacy in the metabolism stabilisation of carbohydrates as compared to not administering it. However, the medical model does not consist in the irruption—and much less in the illegitimate irruption—of medicine in the field of psychotherapy, but rather in the adoption, on the part of the psychotherapists, of a way of thinking and conceiving of the psychotherapeutic process, in the same way that medics conceive of their praxis and, more precisely, their pharmacological treatments, guided by the idea of active, specific principles.

After many years of effort investigating this model in psychotherapy (covering thousands of studies), the meta-analysis of recent years has pulled the tablecloth out from under the medical model: instead of validating the hypothesis and predictions of the medical model, the null hypothesis for each of the mentioned points has been validated, that is, the control hypothesis. The efficacy of psychotherapy depends seventy per cent on "general" factors and just eight per cent on specific, technical factors. From this meta-analysis has arisen what has been called the "contextual model", which emphasises the unspecific aspects of the process (Wampold, 2001).

Belief, consistency and alliance

Given that the efficacy of the specific technical ingredients has been disproved by this large-scale summary of empirical results, it is tempting to think that what has been validated is ambiguity, atmospheric generality, and, ultimately, epistemological chaos and the annihilation of academic and professional psychotherapy. However, nothing of the sort can in fact be concluded. Observing the results, three fundamental phenomena that maintain the efficacy of the psychotherapeutic process can be emphasised: "belief", "consistency", and the "therapeutic alliance". For psychotherapy to be effective, the patient and the therapist must believe firmly in the model to which they adhere, they must be consistent in its application, and, through it, they must engender a working alliance.

It is evident that there is a great paradox here. For psychotherapy to be successful, the therapist *must* believe in the model to which he or she adheres and the patient must *believe* in the therapist and his or her model (inasmuch as it can be discerned). Further, this belief must be incarnated steadfastly throughout the process—this is the consistency aspect. This means that those involved in the process must believe—within a certain range of personal interpretation—in the specific ingredients that the model theoretically prescribes, and must be capable of incarnating these ingredients coherently and personally in the psychotherapeutic action, the only way of holding the therapeutic alliance more or less stable. This means that the contextual model is effective to the extent that we believe in the medical model. It is precisely such belief, and not the specific ingredients as such, which is the factor that best predicts the efficacy of psychotherapy and that, at the same time, grounds the possibility of consistency and alliance, the other two principal predictors of such efficacy. This paradox, ultimately, also explains the equivalence paradox, given that the belief, the consistency, and the alliance are not privileged features of any model in particular.

Given everything just said, it is clear that the contextual model is not a model of specific implicit factors of psychotherapy, that could thus be "extracted" and "purified" theoretically and technically to maximise its effect (and thereby transformed into another aspect of the medical model).

CHAPTER FIVE

Intersubjectivity

We have reflected on some "external" aspects of psycho-therapy, but it is evident that we still do not talk about it appropriately, which, from our perspective, entails a focus on its intimacy. The guiding concept for what follows is the thesis of this essay: that *the psychotherapeutic process is centred in what we could call "the other" or the "not-me"*. There is no doubt that we therapists regularly encounter the "other", which is a part of the not-me and which we have called the "second person". Other aspects of the not-me, such as nature, and other people to whom we do not have any particular bond, are conjugated in the third person.

Intersubjectivity

Despite the abundant production of works regarding the "intersubjec-tive" or "relational" perspectives of the psychotherapies of recent dec-ades, it is difficult to find clear and foundational concepts regarding what intersubjectivity is and how it develops itself in the lives of human beings (Sassenfeld, 2012). To say that intersubjectivity is the ability of tuning, empathizing or bonding with others is not wrong, but it does require development. The reader will be able to see for him or herself whether or not this developing exercise is productive.

So far, in this text, we have tried to bring subjectivity to light. By adding the prefix "inter" we are indicating something very clear: "inter" relates to, in its origin, "interpreter", "medial", "intermediary", "assistant", "agent", "messenger", "negotiator", "sent", and many other similar expressions. It concerns a "between". In the same way that "international" means *between* nations, "intersubjective" means something that occurs "between" subjectivities. We want to emphasise that this is not about a "connection" or "telepathy" or direct harmony, but an intermediate space that requires greater reflection.

To penetrate this phenomenon, we can start with traditions that are close to us. Descartes and Husserl, philosophers we have selected, among others, as references for this book, have an undeniable similarity, despite belonging to very different times, which does not imply that they think in an identical way. The *Metaphysical Meditations* (Descartes, 1980) of Descartes are held up by Husserl in his *Cartesian Meditations* (Husserl, 1979) as an analysis of great quality and refinement. What is common between them is their assertion that subjectivity is the ego as a "monad" (Leibniz, 1980). "Monad", according to the German philosopher Leibniz, refers to each one of the indivisible substances of different natures, gifted in will, that compose the universe. This implies that intersubjectivity requires that two monads relate, link, communicate, or tune to one another. However, monads are singular, unitary structures. In more visual language, we should say that they are "closed" organisations. Varela and Maturana suppose the same, but let us not digress by critiquing this point of view (Maturana & Varela, 1984). At the same time, and derived from the above, the ego, to both authors (there, where the *personal* consciousness is expressed), is an existential trend, a flow of experiences or psychic acts with a narrative history of determined retentions (past) and protentions (future). Thus, the *ego cogitans,* for Descartes, which holds the privilege of absolute epistemological certainty, is the experience of thinking, feeling, wanting, remembering, etc. To reduce the Cartesian *ego cogitans* to cognition, as it is understood today, is entirely wrong and does not withstand even minor analysis. The *ego cogitans,* as we have mentioned, is what we express with verbs, and it seems its occurrence would not be possible originally but as a first person, that is, as a "private" experience. What Husserl adds (among many other points in other dimensions) is that these experiences are *intentional*, that is, they are experiences that relate to "something": it is perception of what is not perception; it is thought about what is not thought; it is feeling something that is not feeling; it is remembering what is not memory. If I perceive a tree, the tree itself is not a perception; if I think of Euclid's fifth axiom, I cannot say that that axiom itself is "thought"; if I feel tenderness for my granddaughter, she is not "my" tenderness; if I remember my mother, she is not "my" memory, but what my memory is about.

However, in all these cases, the acts of perceiving, thinking (understanding), feeling, or remembering are seemingly unapproachable for others. Nobody has direct access to my thoughts, my memories or my emotions. This "my" regards everything that occurs addressed as "me"; "I" am the one who experiences and feels, and I am apart and isolated from the "other". I am a monad. Further, all of this applies the other way around also: I do not have direct access to the existential trend of others.

However, the exit from this intersubjective paradox, that is, when trying to open a hole in structures that these authors define as closed, so as to generate in this way a bond and an identification (empathy, compassion, etc.), takes very different directions in Descartes and in Husserl.

Descartes turns to God whereas Husserl turns to, what he calls, "analogue apperception". Before discussing these exits, it is important to consider a prior question. On what grounds is it thought that these exits are necessary? If we are monads and *certainly* monads, what sense is there in twisting the concept with which we have begun our reflection so as to, precisely, transform it into a denial of itself (monads not monads)? Descartes says: "How do I know that the persons I see from my balcony are not toys actioned by springs?" For his part, Husserl asks himself: "How do I know that the other is *other* and not a thing?" They both set out the problem in much more elaborated contexts but, essentially, they ask themselves the same question. Maybe the answer to this question is too simple and obvious for some philosophers to bother considering: Descartes and Husserl ask themselves *because* they know those pedestrians *are not* toys, because they know *they are others* and not things. They know, but have no "explanation" nor can understand that knowledge. That is why they must investigate and ask the question.

In his epistemological concepts, Descartes supports himself in what he considers the only possible certainty: it does not matter if I am tricked regarding what I think things are, if I am dreaming them, if I am hallucinating everything I think, perceive, feel, remember, etc., the only evidence is that which happens to me. From this insight comes the famous phrase *ego cogito, ergo sum*; fairly, it should be translated as "I experience, therefore I exist". This phrase has suffered bad interpretations, re-interpretations, bad understandings, de-contextualisations and much more. We will not enter into this story here, although is notable and worthy of being read, told and understood.

However, the problem of otherness is not just the "world in general", which at first sight seemed undeniable and certainly "not-me", but also and more particularly these persons that walk down the street that Descartes knows are not toys moved by springs. That is to say, these persons fall under the specification we designate as "the" other and, no matter how much we try, we cannot conjugate these persons in the neutral third person. These others are not "things" ("it") but others like me who experience themselves, that is, they are each a first person, which is not the case for the tree nor the river that crosses the city. But, on the other hand, if the only solid, truthful, undoubtable entity is *my* ego in exercise, we have been left alone, isolated, genuinely monadic. How does Descartes recover evidence for the world and, especially, for the "other"? He asks God for help, which is always a good choice for a believer. To include God in this matter, he must prove first that God exists. It is not necessary to reproduce that argument here, but let us suppose that it is successful. Then, if God created me, he also created the others and the world, and that is why they are there for me and I am for them. This extra philosophical exit was called the *deus ex machina*, that is, a God that does not come from the field of Descartes' methodological deductions, but from an "outside" related to belief.

Hegel (1966), who we will not consider here except as a distant reference, given that his "system" is a linguistic and conceptual jungle that takes much time to master, would say: "The other is the one who allows me to be me". If this is so, it is clear why Descartes and Husserl must rescue the other and, with him, intersubjectivity, as it is the only way I can be me.

Husserl takes a different road from Descartes and employs a device we could term "expansion": the other, of whom we are aware, always presents an "excess", a beyond (plus) what we observe or directly perceive. That is, the other does not fit into the category of the neutral third person. When I am presented with a person I do not perceive just his or her aspect as a living thing (that all living things naturally have), but also a person with a consciousness, a psychic life, succinctly, one who is *like* me: Husserl calls this "apperception". Why is it, for me, that the condition of the other is an excess, something that goes beyond perceptual "data"? In this regard Husserl is not especially clear, repeating with different words the same thought. The "apperception" is an "appresentation" that requires a core of "presentation". It is an "appresentation" linked and merged by associations to the "presentation", what he calls "co-perception". The perception and apperception operate as a unit, "as if I was (my essential nature) 'there', in the place of the physical organic body of 'other', given to me as 'there' and to the other as 'here'" (Husserl, 1979, p. 192). All this experience occurs in my monad, while always being it, given that knowledge of the other is not tantamount to having access to his or her existential trend, as much as we know he or she has it.

I recognise that this starting point is confusing and could be widely extended, but with the same confusion, in a thorough study of Husserl's thought. However, all such confusion, as much as it extends or reduces, does not in itself permit greater clarity in the initial verification of the other as such, that is, of something "strange" (not-me), but *like me*.

For his part, Sartre (1966), like Hegel, thinks we need the other to confirm our own identity, and specifies something very similar to Hegel's figure of the master and slave. For Sartre, the existing human has liberty and, therefore, relations with the other are always of conflict, given that one will try to own the other's liberty, and vice versa. But the existence of the other is not a hypothesis, it is not a conjecture. This statement is grounded in an obvious situation: the other makes him or herself present, not as an object, but as a subject, or subjectivity, which implies his or her liberty regarding his or her valuations, projects, personal situation, etc. It is not about a "theory" (as the term "theory of mind" might suggest) but a certainty. This obviousness is a common experience based, in a fundamental way, on an extraordinarily common phenomenon: *the look*. When the other looks at us we perceive in him or her not an object, of which we would have no reason to be afraid or which we could use as a "resource" without consequence. Rather, we find that, behind that look, there is a subjectivity. There is a protagonist of the looking, a being from whom we can expect things (complicity, solidarity, pleasure, understanding, confrontation, obstacles to our goals, etc.). However, the most surprising thing is that the look of the other makes us conscious of ourselves through feelings that occur in us, that are precisely and paradigmatically human and that take such a look as their prerequisite: embarrassment, shyness, humiliation, and pride, among others.

CHAPTER SIX

The suspended ego: an approach to Buddhism

The inspiration for this chapter, and some quotations, are taken from Brazier's *Buddhist Psychology: Liberate your mind, embrace life* (Brazier, 2003). What makes Buddhism so attractive to disciplines like psychology and psychotherapy? The answer is simple, clear, and direct: what makes it attractive is that it has to do with human suffering and the way in which we confront it. The search for serenity, calm, and wisdom in the experience of existing, that is, of a life without suffering or worry, appears as an obvious and desirable objective universally. However, suffering is unavoidable. What, then, can we do? If we cannot suppress suffering, we must channel it, provide it with an orientation, and maybe a sense. How can this be done? In the daily life of any person who lives in a big city, or who practises any activity of labour under the dynamic of commercial relations that govern us, the answer is clear: by creating a strong identity and obtaining power, autonomy, success, money, status, and the like. In this pursuit, efficiency, competence, promptness, and productivity are the means of success. However, that is not the only answer. There are others, although it is not difficult to see the tendency of our culture, enveloped in a strange, abusive, and self-destructing idea of development, to "recover" and "assimilate" other ways of conceiving human life that

49

contradict this. Effectively, Buddhism can quickly be transformed into a trend or a consumer product. We will attempt here to skip these psychological and political complexities, not because we consider them irrelevant, but because adequate reflection on them requires, first, that we understand what we are talking about. In order to do so, and then to focus on its applications to psychotherapy, we will refer directly to the fundamental teaching of the Buddha Siddhartha Gautama. Maybe the old philosophical habit of going to the source is here, again, a good methodological approach.

The ideas and the practice

Buddhism is not just a practice, but a practice expressed in diverse oral and written teachings (*sutras*). The expression *Buddha* means, in Sanskrit, "intelligent" or "visionary". It comes from the verb *budh*, which means "to wake up", "to pay attention", "to realise", "to understand", or "to recover consciousness after a faint". According to Buddhism, Buddha is the title assigned to those individuals who have made their nature *bodi*, that is, they have "woken up" and made themselves conscious. The Buddha lived between the sixth and fifth centuries BC, the same period in which the basis of occidental culture was founded in Greece. The oral tradition of the teachings of the Buddha was captured many centuries later in written texts called *sutras*, originally in Pali (one of the most ancient Indo-European languages) in a text known as The Pali Canon. Later on, these teachings were translated into Sanskrit. Siddhartha Gautama is considered "the Buddha of our era". It is necessary to emphasise that "Buddha" is not a proper name, but an adjective (meaning "illuminated"), and this is why Siddhartha Gautama is called *"the* Buddha". It is also important to mention that Buddhism is considered by many of its followers to be a non-theistic "religion", which does not fit well with the occidental conception of religion. In Buddhism, strictly, there is no god. Rather, it concerns matters linked to the human being and the whole of nature. Therefore, the Buddha merely represents an example, acting as a guide and a teacher for those beings who must take the path alone so as to achieve spiritual awakening and to see truth and reality as they are. It is about understanding the true nature of the mind and the world, and such understanding may be discovered by anybody if the right path is followed. However, long ago, occidental thought from its Graeco-Roman root has maintained that reality as such is inaccessible to human beings. This conviction does not arise only from the radical constructivism of our time, which we have mentioned in passing, nor from what is confusingly called postmodernity, but rather it reaches back to Plato and, in the modern period, to Kant, Descartes, and the other leading lights of Western philosophy. It is enough to remember the Kantian distinction between "phenomenon" (the approachable) and "noumenon" (the thing "itself", which is unapproachable).

The Buddha

The life of Siddhartha Gautama is fundamental to the origin of his experiential postulates. (How could it be otherwise?) Wisdom has to do with experience of life. As we mentioned, Prince Siddhartha Gautama was born at the end of the sixth century BC. His mother died when he was born, and the first twenty-nine years of his life went by completely devoid of spiritual activity. He lived with his family throughout this time, married, and had at least one child. His life was one of much luxury and comfort. He received the best education and training possible in his time. At the age of twenty-nine, however, he began to feel curious about how things were in the external world and asked his father, Suddhodana, for permission to satisfy his interest. Suddhodana agreed, but prepared for his son's journey by ordering that the streets be cleared of all sights that might trouble the overprotected awareness of the prince. Yet these careful arrangements failed as Siddhartha, met by crowds when passing through the streets, could not avoid perceiving pain in its most intense forms in what has since been termed the "Four Encounters": the first three, sickness, aging, and death (the body scripts, we might say), and the fourth, an ascetic, the meaning of which is different from the first three, as we will see presently. Siddhartha realised that he, like any other person, would be subject to the same suffering, and his mood turned sombre, asking himself how somebody can live in peace and happiness if this is what life brings. If growing old, becoming ill, and dying is what every human being must face, all that constitutes the foundation of suffering is, then, unavoidable. It is clear how these paradigmatic situations of suffering indicate the finite nature of the human being and the inevitable end of existence. Siddhartha, worried by what he had seen, understood that he had remained apart, separated from the life of human beings, encapsulated in a false world, and, therefore, that his nature had remained anaesthetised. He thus made a radical decision: he would separate from his father, his wife, and his little son, and, along with that, from all the conveniences of the palace and all of his possessions. He decided, then, to follow the path of the ascetic seen in the Four Encounters, but in a more radical version, adopting the life of the monks who lived as beggars and lacked all material property.

After a long search, suffering due to hunger, cold, pain, and sickness, Siddhartha came to understand four phenomena that would explain the way in which human beings experience life. These phenomena arrived to him one confusing and desperate night, suddenly and all together. They have since been called the "Four Noble Truths". Without beginning from these four pillars, one will not be able to understand what Buddhism is. Yet, these are not premises or theoretical postulates, but rather phenomena open to experience by anybody and self-evident. We might, thus, call them a set of experiential axioms.

Dukkha

The first noble truth (*dukkha*) holds what we have already said: that in the lives of human beings suffering is unavoidable. We cannot live without suffering. Naturally, not all sufferings are permanent, nor equal, but a life without suffering is unimaginable.

Going to the source, this noble truth is described in Samyutta Nikaya 61.11.5, third section of Pali Sutras, as follows: "birth, old age, sickness, death, grief, lamentation, pain, depression, and agitation are *dukkha*. *Dukkha* is being associated with what you do not like, being separated from what you do like, and not being able to get what you want" (Brazier, 2003, p. 10).

A long explanation is not required to prove that it is the same suffering that we, as psychotherapists, see daily. However, while human beings do not experience suffering as an isolated and unique entity, each instance of suffering generates the deepest and most heart-rending emotions: physical damage makes us writhe in pain; moral damage, in indignation; danger, in fear or terror; the idea of death, in anguish; passionate love, in desperation. When I say "writhe" I mean a violent, deforming twist of one's entire being. Put briefly, the Buddha found that suffering awakens strong reactions in us. Such emotional reactions were, in turn, termed *samudaya*, the second noble truth.

Samudaya

The noble truth of *samudaya*, as an answer to affliction, is described in Samyutta Nikaya 56.11.6: "The noble truth of *samudaya*, response to affliction, is this: it is thirst for self re-creation that is associated with greed. It lights upon whatever pleasures are to be found here and there. It is thirst for sense-pleasure, for being and for non-being" (Brazier, 2003, p. 11).

This seems simple and clear, but it is necessary to specify a few terms. In using the expression "thirst" the Buddha refers to a state of great intensity that wants only to be satisfied (the cessation of the suffering). The English translation of the Sanskrit word *trishna* is a familiar expression in the field of addictions: "craving". For its part, "re-creation" refers to the attempt to return to being the person we believe we were before the suffering, a kind of "normalisation", "reaffirmation" and "stabilisation" of what we suppose defines us in a substantive way. The suffering motivates the search for relief and, as we mentioned, comes with great emotional intensity. What do we want? We want to be eternal, we want eternal youth, and we want the absence of illness, loss, depression, and anxiety. That is, we want permanence, infinity, security, and stability. We know that this is impossible, but in diverse and foolish ways we insist on it. This impossibility is the fundamental source of suffering.

The emotions produced by this situation can be channelled in two main directions: the first is directed to the addicted thirst, that searches for immediate relief, and that is usually destructive and, paradoxically, thanatic. The second, as we will see presently, is a path that leads to overcoming, construction, and the vital "nobleness". We should not confuse this "nobleness" with some aristocratic ambition, as it is in fact exactly the opposite and strongly linked to ethics, which we will see later on. The addiction is the attachment to things, situations, and persons that transitorily relieve our suffering (power, money, sex, belongings, substances, food, persons, etc.). If we succeed in adhering to these things, situations, and persons, and we thus become dependent on them such that, if they are missing, it produces suffering in us, a circuit of positive feedback is closed (the more you have, the more you want) and is precisely that which we call addiction.

The surprising thing that Buddhism suggests is that the set of patterns of avoidance of suffering, as they repeat iteratively and innumerably, forms a complex scheme that takes more definite shape and consistency over time and, so to speak, starts to "define" the person, establishing his or her features, habits, and repetitions such that, in a moment, his or her life takes on the appearance of something determined, solid, and stable. This is what Buddhism terms "self". This self is ultimately metaphorically gaoled as the Buddha was in his palace, preventing him from seeing beyond the palace to the other, the not-me, what is by itself and what does not refer to us. Thus, the self and its unavoidable self-reference is, for Buddhism, the supreme addiction or the maximum prison.

Nirodha

The second possible direction of the emotions, or energy, released by suffering, is that oriented towards the above-mentioned noble path, which is contained in the third truth: *nirodha*.

The description of the noble truth *nirodha* in Samyutta Nikaya 61.11.7 is: "The noble truth of *nirodha*, containment, is this: it is the complete capturing of that thirst. It is to let go of, be liberated from and refuse to dwell in the object of that thirst" (Brazier, 2003, p. 13).

The control and channelling of that energy require firstly that we free ourselves of the things and situations to which we have become addicted, that we stop inhabiting them, understanding that this inhabiting proceeds from "habit" and that, among other effects, hides from us the addicted underlying nature, taking an innocent and naive appearance. However, it is enough to offer an obstacle to some of our habits to appreciate the power that underlies them. When breaking free of that inhabiting, the suffering again becomes evident: it is this energy that Buddhism proposes we channel, lead, and tame, in order to arrive at the fourth noble truth: *marga*.

Marga

"The noble truth of *Marga*, the right track is this: it is the noble eight limb way, namely right view, right thought, right speech, right action, right livelihood, right effort, right mindfulness, right *Samadhi*" (Sanyutta Nikaya 61.11.8, cited in Brazier, 2003, p. 15).

The expression "right", essential to this noble truth, could also be expressed as "correct", not merely of adequate "measure" but of an ethical and moral value. What is "right" is what does "justice" in the measure of each thing, permitting its natural flow. In the second place, *marga* is not something we impose on things by a magnanimous or generous act, but something that is in the things themselves. For its part, "right awareness" is what is known as "mindfulness" (in Sanskrit, *smriti*), meaning "to perceive without catching" or to take an object into account with "reverent attention".

It is evident that we cannot connect these Buddhist ideas directly to practices in psychotherapy, but we must instead first perform a preliminary analysis.

CHAPTER SEVEN

Naga

A *naga* is a semi-divine serpent with a human face, generally that of a woman. Measuring between three and six metres in length, nagas are said to be beings of cold blood, with pretty scales, and big, bright, almost luminescent eyes, that live as water serpents in a watery region of Pakistan. Popular tradition alleges that nagas are very intelligent, wise and patient, and have great charm, making them very powerful without the need to turn to violence. They prepare traps in their territory for intruders, whom they attack first with magic and, at the end, with their poisonous bite.

An interesting *sutra*, called "The Anthill" (Vammika Sutta, MN 23), refers to a dream of one of the Buddha's followers named Kassapa. The most surprising aspect of this *sutra* is the way in which the Buddha interprets the dream. Kassapa is in front of the anthill. With a knife, he penetrates the mound from which the anthill is formed and finds, respectively, the following objects: an obstacle (barrier), a toad, a forked path, a strainer, a turtle, an axe and a tree trunk, a piece of meat and, finally, a naga, the serpent. The Buddha interprets that the anthill represents the body and its structure of change and impermanence. The knife represents the wisdom that allows for the dissection in search of the truth and the cutting of illusory constructions, trespassing each one of the layers of the mind and releasing the energy underlying each one by separating them from their corresponding habits. The barrier represents denial, the refusal to look, the complete resistance against letting go of habits and the avoidance of all self-examination, pretending everything is fine. The toad represents desperation due to anger and resentment that lies hidden and camouflaged. The forked path symbolises indecision, the lack of commitment necessary for spiritual progress. The strainer represents what is retained from the river-flow, the five impurities or obstacles: hedonism, sloth, hostility, paralysing worry, and unhealthy doubt. The turtle stands for the creation of a protective self, as hard as its shell. The axe and the tree trunk symbolise, respectively, the act of searching with violence and the power of habit. The meat, for its part, represents lust. The ninth and final symbol found in the anthill is the most profound and fundamental: the naga. In his dream, Kassapa discovers the serpent that, on one hand, represents energy and healing (as in the symbol of medicine, formed by a serpent and a staff), the liberation of attachments and spirituality, and, on the other hand, a great danger, the lethal poison. That is, the naga serpent can be either healing or destructive. To put it in other words, for the Buddha, in the foundation of our mind there is only one energy principle, which can be used for either healing or for destruction. *Dukkha*, suffering, generates anguish and releases energy, and that energy is the naga, in the sense that it can be channelled in the path of the creation of a defensive self, armed on the basis of addictions, attachments, and avoidances that are condemned to failure—given that suffering is inescapable—or else channelled and oriented to *marga* and enlightenment, that is, to the eightfold path. It is on this path that the Buddhist ethic becomes evident.

The ethics and the practice

The noble eightfold path is considered the way that leads to the capacity for reducing and coexisting with *dukkha* (suffering). The essential point is the effort to ignore the desire to appropriate, but to see "the other" (nature, persons, thoughts, emotions, and situations), effectively as *not-me*, as *not-self*, and allowing all that emerges in its own nature. Undoubtedly, we are a part of a totality of what there is, but we are not owners of anything. What makes understanding of this idea more difficult is our rooted conviction that we have an internal world that belongs to us and that comprises what we are, and that certain things of the world and others belong to us (such as *my* house, *my* children, *my* objects). Another point is made with regard to the body. How can we be owners of a body formed by atoms as ancient as the ones present in the first stages of the universe many billions of years ago?

The elements of the noble eightfold path are subdivided into three aspects: wisdom, ethical behaviour, and mind training (or meditation). Within all the elements of the noble path, the word "right" or "straight" is a translation of the word *samm*, which means "summit", "coherence", or "perfection".

The eightfold path

We will briefly mention the fundamental aspects of this path. Right view or understanding refers to the comprehension of the Four Noble Truths of Buddhism, that is, that suffering exists and that its origin is in the desire for permanence (youth, absence of illness and death). It is necessary to understand that everything is impermanent, brief and changing.

Right thought or right determination consists in allowing things to flow under the conviction that nothing is constant. Besides, it implies the intention of good faith and the will of no violence towards living organisms. It is separated from cruelty, having in its place goodness and compassion.

For its part, ethical behaviour (*shila*) includes right speech, consisting of abstention from lying and from slanderous, defamatory, disrespectful, or frivolous speech. To abstain from participating in these forms of speech means, naturally, that we must speak the truth and use friendly words that are meaningful and useful.

Right action implies a series of abstentions: from taking life, from taking what has not been given to us, that is, from stealing, and from inappropriate and harmful sensual behaviour.

Right livelihood consists in the foundation or means of survival being based on the concept of harmlessness or "non-damage" (*ahimsa*), which essentially declares that we should not choose trades or professions which, directly or indirectly, cause harm to other living beings or the world in general. We should not trade lethal weapons, toxic drinks, or poisons. Even less should we trade in humans: a prohibition covering the slave trade, prostitution, corruption, swindles, tricks, robbery, intrigue, and persuasion that undervalues others. Additionally, in a relevant way, we should abstain from making profit from speculation.

Right effort is part of what can be grouped under the concept of mind training (*samādhi*). This Sanskrit word has been subject to a variety of translations, the foremost of which are: "meditation", "concentration", "mental discipline", "mind and heart nurturing", and "being present". We prefer, however, the version we have mentioned above: *to perceive without catching*, or *to perceive reverentially,* given the implication of acknowledging nature and measuring everything and every person in itself, without pretending that we could be the ones who provide such dimensions. It involves continuous effort and constant practice of, in essence, keeping the mind free of thoughts that could harm the ability to do or put into practice the other elements of the noble path. Right effort has also been called "diligence" or "right energy", consisting in preventing ill health that has not yet appeared and making efforts to dismiss the ill health that has already appeared; correspondingly, making efforts to produce the health that has not yet appeared and making efforts to cultivate the health that has already appeared.

Basically, then, the eightfold path consists in the attentive, reverent, and conscious contemplation of the body, of others, of one's surroundings, of the mind, and of the thoughts.

CHAPTER EIGHT

The mind

W hat is the structure of the mind proposed by the Buddha? Maybe it is in this point that it becomes evident to us that our ordinary concepts of mind can be perfectly illusory. The mind, for the Buddha, is a point, or a virtuality, in which the sensorial afferents intersect. As we have outlined, Descartes, contemporary psychology, and many others, have thought the same: the mind configures, structures, and establishes itself on the basis of environmental afferents. We all know that these afferents come from the five sense organs, but what is a sense organ? It is something that receives or, in words of the Buddha, that is "visited" by the otherness, the not-me: our ear is visited by sounds; our eyes by lights, colours, and shapes; our sense of taste by flavours; our sense of smell by scents, and so on. The essential difference is that, for the Buddha, the senses are not five, but six. The sixth is *mano-vijnana,* which is visited by thoughts, feelings, fantasies and memories (Fig. 1). That is, what we call the "conscious" mind is, in fact, another sense organ. There is in this a certain surprise: if we see a tree, it is evident that we do not say that we have generated that tree, that we are that tree and, therefore, that it belongs to us, yet we do say this of our thoughts, memories, fantasies, and feelings, supposing that we created them and that we maintain dominance over them. A simple exercise proposed by Caroline Brazier (2003) can help us to prove this: sit for twenty minutes in a café and put on the table a sheet of paper with six columns, corresponding to the traditional sense organs plus the "mind". Mark with an "x" each time you notice something you heard, saw, remembered, felt, smelled, thought, grieved for, disliked, etc. When the time is up, look at the sheet and ask what, of all that, was planned or guided by you. You will confirm that all its contents, including the mental and corporeal, merely "got to you". We experience these stimuli in the first person, it is true, but we are not the owners of these stimuli; we do not control what of that experience arrives.

With good reason, we can refute that the mind "builds" the afferents in accordance with its own organisation and structural coupling, and that the tree is not something in "itself" that can visit us via a neutral sense organ acting as a mere receptacle. That explanation can be right from many angles, but not all. What we experience is not that explanation, nor the integration of a perception performed in the visual cortex. To confuse these levels generates a form of *hypostasis*, that is, the idea that our theoretical constructs are real, that whatever was thought before was illusory but that now, finally, we have the true explanation.

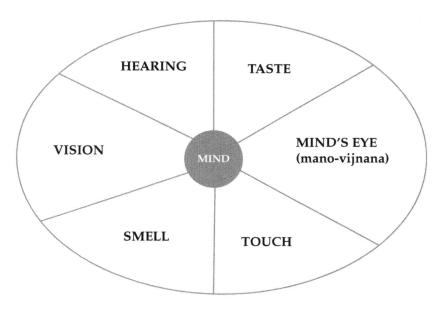

Figure 1. Six senses model (six vijnana).

In medicine, and especially in psychiatry and psychotherapy, hypostasis has had serious practical consequences when applying techniques to persons based on taking theories to be real. The idea that mental disorders were a "hyper-affectivity" and that "affectivity" was produced by the frontal lobe, for instance, were grounds for the performance of over 10,000 lobotomies in the 1930s and 1940s in the United States. It is enough to review any piece of scientific history to confirm that, in each time and for every theory, it has been believed that true "reality" has been finally apprehended. However, paradoxically, what is being affirmed repeatedly is that such reality does not exist, including the supposed reality of scientific theories. It is necessary to ask ourselves, then, why it is that we believe there is a "world itself". Even still, that question is wrongly formulated as the "why" suggests a casual answer, which is usually a dead end. In our experience there is a reality—the tree is there, independent of our perception—although we cannot explain why it happens like this, or even how it occurs this way. What has to be explained, theorised and investigated requires, as a starting point, the phenomena, that is, the way of the experience, rather than believing that the experience should adjust with explanation. The only means of consistently reflecting on experience is by using other experiences, not with constructs or theoretical models that, usually, lose the sense of the obvious. It will be said against this point, and with good reason, that the sun does not travel around the Earth. Yet that will never be an experience. We say "the sun came out" and not "the Earth turned". These two levels of knowledge are different and we cannot lose sight of that difference without losing sight also of the way in which we experience ourselves and the world in the midst of which we live. Nobody experiences their own hepatic metabolism, which is not to say that we cannot have knowledge of it, but rather it is knowledge that we should not confuse with the experiences in which we live. In the same way, death is a natural and calm biochemical event, but this is not how we experience its possibility and reality while consciousness lasts.

The skandhas

How does this Buddhist mind operate in regards to the afferents, then? That is, regarding what gets to us as the other?

Observing the diagram (Fig. 2), we can see that it is a circle rather than a linear system starting at one point and reaching another. It is

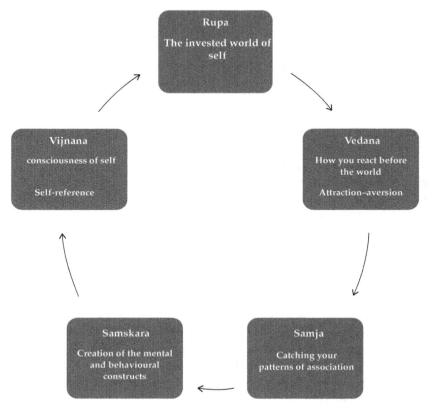

Figure 2. Skandhas.

about positive feedback, unlike the majority of corporeal functions with reflexive circuits. In a metaphorical sense, the result is, at the same time, the cause. It is interesting to emphasise, therefore, that the point of beginning and ending, for Buddhism, is designated with the Sanskrit word *rupa*. *Rupa* is something that appears to consciousness, similar to the concept of a "phenomenon", as seen previously, but that accepts from the beginning the distortion of that appearance. That distortion may be affirmed because it is possible to eliminate it. *Rupa* is always something "other" received in an inappropriate way (in the sense of not being exactly what it is). What produces this distortion? The ego, or, expressed in a better way, the fiction or story of what we believe to be the self-referent lens, which watches the world and others in a disrupted and altered way, as through a disfiguring glass. The extreme case of this phenomenon is delusional "perception": the world and the others in it are always with me at the centre; they are supported only by *my* presence; they refer *to me,* they speak to *me,* they mean something directly related to *my ego.* There is no neutrality nor causality and, accordingly, there is no understanding that others, in their spontaneity and liberty, unfold in multiple directions in which we are just exceptionally included as ego. This perspective would be indisputable if there were no other experiences to cast serious doubts on it. It has been termed the "judgement" of reality, the real, the sense of reality, and other similar and not necessarily happy expressions (Ojeda, 1987).

For Buddhism, *rupa* is the otherness "invested" of ego, that is, with a coefficient of me (my) added, which is inappropriate for that other. This leads to a certain reaction in us that can be of attraction or aversion. Given our tendency to create behavioural habits and the incessant repetition that they imply, disfigured perception clings more and more tightly to our conviction, increasing the probability that, given a new presentation of the same object, person, or situation, the distorted perception will reinforce itself. It is in this process that the "mind", understood as ego, is created, a historical and biographical process whose netting becomes denser with each iteration of the above. This implies the creation of a "view" of the world and the otherness, which is very difficult to break and becomes more complicated each time, inhibiting each thing, situation, or person (the otherness) from showing its own true dimension and nature. In other words, the "personal" appreciation of the otherness correlates to what we believe to be "myself" and, therefore, it determines the way in which we approach the world, and our valuation and perception of that approach. The circuit thus closes in on itself and leaves very little space for the freedom, precisely, of that otherness.

As is seen in the above diagram, Buddhism expresses in Sanskrit the complex system I have just exposed. Many other related concepts and nuances will not be elucidated just yet, including, for example, the more clearly behavioural aspects of the process (such as *karma*).

CHAPTER NINE

Psychotherapeutic change

We have all read and heard that psychotherapy seeks a "change" in the patient and great effort is expended to discover the factors that engender such change. But we also know that change, paradoxically, is the only permanent condition of anything, including us, others, and nature in its entirety. It is necessary to ask ourselves, then, what kind of change we, in psychotherapy, mean. Allow me to recount an exercise developed by Caroline Brazier, which is to be performed in psychotherapy study groups. To start, fifty "psychological" concepts are listed, such as envy, generosity, collaboration, aggression, autonomy, dependence, honesty, competitiveness, solidarity, loyalty, manipulation, servility, etc. The group, with no major difficulty or controversy, categorises these concepts as either "desirable" or "undesirable" features in a person (not necessarily only in relation to therapeutic objectives). As a result, something remarkable becomes apparent—that the social and cultural world in the West works essentially on the basis of those concepts that have been placed in the non-desirable list. Effectively, a world that is individualist, competitive, dishonest, non-collaborative, and violent (among many other features) is designated as undesirable by this group (along with many other groups and individuals). How is it possible, then, for that world, created by all of us as a society, to be so different from what we desire and what we believe privately? That simple contradiction (which is easy to confirm) has complex consequences and important ethical dimensions. In our trade as psychotherapists, should we aim at facilitating persons, following the above social valuations, to become warriors capable of facing that unscrupulous jungle or, guided by what appears desirable, to develop a "maladjustment" to that environment and thus a vulnerability with serious practical consequences? How can we guide ourselves in this decision? Do we not tend to think that features such as a strong mental structure, independence, success, and self-sufficiency are desirable as objectives in psychotherapy? This problem is ethical and is played out within our professional field, though we usually think and speak little about it.

As we have mentioned, permanent change and transformation, indicated in Greek by the word *metabolé*, seems to be the only "constant" in all that exists and in all persons. The question, then, is no longer how to produce changes, but, essentially, how to help the patient to channel his or her process of vital change (the progression through the different stages of life). We used to think that human suffering could be calmed by fixing, rigidising, and repeating that which apparently conjures the change. Thus, detaching the apparent ritual detention through repetition consists in placing the person again in the field in which the primary suffering occurred.

Caroline Brazier (Brazier, 2003, p. 13), following David Brazier's conceptualisations, points out that the common meaning of the word *nirodha* is not just a "cessation" but a harnessing, that is, an instrument that allows us to orient and conduct the transforming movement that we do not create and that we cannot avoid. It is because of this that what I or any other colleague can think in this sense—that is, the direction we believe to be correct and in which we try to encourage the therapeutic change—does not seem to be, necessarily, a reliable mould for guiding our work. Do we, as psychotherapists, have a *model* of what a human being should be? It seems we do. However, it is enough to review the more than 300 "mental disorders" that are included in the fifth edition of the *Diagnostic and Statistical Manual of Mental Disorders* (American Psychiatric Association, 2013) to prove that this regulation is not just capricious but, frankly, abusive. To my understanding, this occurs because we have the pretence to knowledge of what the person needs, what adaptation is required, and what "normality" is, and, further, the arrogance of believing that we can impose all these concepts on people who suffer and seek our professional help. As we will promptly see, nobody can decide this kind of issue for another. However, it would be blind to say that there are no persons suffering from very severe "disorders" that break the frame of these considerations. A person who suffers from dementia, or schizophrenia in a devastating stage, or severe mood exaltation and anxiety, among other "disorders", is deeply altered in anybody's understanding. It is to them that an important part of the psychiatric effort is dedicated. Yet that spectrum of deviations from normality is confined and does not comprise all those who most frequently turn to psychotherapy. This is well known to all psychotherapists.

Nevertheless, we operate as if the ethical perspective of therapeutic goals were obvious and resolvable by means of experts' agreements. The trend of "adapters" has been called into question many times but, in these critical attempts, they tend to be marginalised and considered as exotic minorities that defy the central power of the organisations that govern the exercise of the profession. These organisations are frequently highly linked to economic or academic powers (universities and hegemonic publications) that are very difficult to counteract. We have mentioned this point in detail in other publications, especially in regard to the contemporary psychiatric situation with respect to the pharmaceutical industry and its clear connection to medical organisations, or what are called "specialist scientific societies". This phenomenon tends to be less evident in psychotherapy, but is present nevertheless. We merely mention this connection here, as it is not the main theme of this essay, though with an understanding that this argument might be enforced at any point.

The self, the ego, and the myself revisited

Self is a commonly-used word in English. Thus, for example, we say: "she's back to her old *self* again", which is, in Spanish, "*ella ha vuelto a ser* la misma *de antes*", or "she bought a dress with a *self*-belt", which translates into Spanish as "*se compró un vestido con cinturón de la* misma *tela*". We can also say "you're still the same old *self*, then", which is, in Spanish, "*entonces, todavía eres el* mismo *de antes*". It is used in compound words to provide emphasis: myself (*mí mismo*), yourself (*tú mismo*), ourselves (*nosotros mismos*) and yourselves (*ustedes mismos*). It is evident that "self" could not be translated into Spanish without the expression *mismo* ("same"). Similar words are used in classical and contemporary languages. In Greek we find *"to autos"*, from which expressions such as "autonomy", "authority", and "authorship" are derived. In Latin, the expression *"idem"* gives rise to many English words, such as "identical" and "identity". In German, the word is *"Selbst"*, which is used very similarly to the English. If we reflect on these words for a moment we discover something remarkable. For something to be *"lo mismo"* (the same) a "re-knowledge" is necessary: this book is the same as the one I was reading yesterday; the "same attitude" is that which happened before; I am the same person as I was a week ago; this house is the same that I bought five years ago. Without this aspect of "experience again", the *mismidad* ("selfness") would disappear. For how could I say that something I experience for the first time is somehow "the same"? It is possible that it would be similar to something that occurred before, but it is not *"lo mismo"* (the same). Therefore, to try to understand the fact that I consider myself *"el mismo"* (the same) over the course of my life, it is necessary that there be a "re-membering". The *mismo* ("same") is the "again", that which occurred before. What is not susceptible to being "re-known" as having been, that which does not have a history of itself, cannot be, in its first appearance, *"lo mismo"* ("the same"). However, if I say my friend Marco *is* my friend Marco, that is, that he is the *mismo* ("same"), it is because I "re-know" him even though he is now bald and his beard is greyish. The same does not imply invariability but, rather, a determined and essential configuration. It seems that the experience resists getting tangled in details and the "eidetic reduction" described in previous chapters is completely spontaneous. The song "Yesterday" can be interpreted in very different ways but it does not, on that account, stop being "the same" (*la misma*).

To the extent that it necessarily implies the memory, the *"mí mismo"* ("myself") is historical and biographical. Perhaps a brief clinical excursus will allow us to clarify what it is we are trying to express. The degenerative primary diseases of the brain, such as Alzheimer's disease, are characterised by a loss of the ability to remember, first, recent events and, as the degeneration develops, more and more distant events. Along with this, and among many other symptoms, the person affected presents characteristic disorientation: he or she gets lost in streets that were once familiar, does not know how to get back home, and confuses the time in which he or she is living. At a more advanced stage, the sufferer does not recognise their own family and eventually no longer recognises him or herself—he or she does not know who he or she is. Naturally, the process is much more complex than this simple outline, but it is enough for our present purposes.

Strictly, the patient suffering from Alzheimer's disease in its later stages, cannot answer the question "who" because they can no longer remember, or bring to presence, the before-been (Ojeda, 1998) (the absent) and, therefore, they have no history. It is evident then that a being without a history does not possess the *mismidad* ("selfness") that determines "who I am" and, further, all the conjugations that contain the "I am" (otherwise, all, and always) as its anchoring. We can confirm that the personal history we call biography is not something that is owned just due to the fact of having happened but rather due to the fact of making itself present, that is, the permanent implicit or explicit presence of the before-been in our present. If the past stops being present in its having been (in its absent presence), the person loses their who, their *mismidad* ("selfness"). Nevertheless, in no way does the consciousness cease existing: it is not the same comatose state as Alzheimer's disease.

The writer Nicole Krauss, in her beautiful novel entitled *Man Walks into a Room* (Krauss, 2002), presents an adult character who has lost all his memories from the age of twelve due to a neurosurgical intervention:

> The forgetting was beyond his control [...] It angered him to have so little choice in his own fate—to go to sleep in the liberty of childhood and to wake up twenty-four years later in a life he had nothing to do with, surrounded by people who expected him to be someone he felt he'd never been [...] With sleeping came forgetfulness. He felt at home there. (Krauss, 2002, p. 25)

The ego

In Latin, *ego* means "I". For "the same", as we have mentioned, the expression *idem* is used. But what does "I" mean? Do we use it to express any person? Evidently, no. If I say "I", I am performing some kind of apheresis and I am saying "myself", "this, who I am", "I do not mean anybody, but myself". With respect to the above considerations, then, we can then say that *self, ego, idem*, and *I* are one and the *same* thing. Going forward, we will adopt the expression "ego" to refer to all of these concepts that form, in an ordinary and broad sense, personal identity.

That the ego is historical means that it is constituted through time and that its story is held by the memory. We should thus ask ourselves about the memory. We have already mentioned that to "re-member" is to bring to presence the before-been, what was but is no longer and, therefore, the presence of which is to us given via something that re-presents it, but is not that property itself, what we have called "imago" or "representative". If I remember that yesterday I was reading Fernando Pessoa, this act is different from the act of reading him right now. The mode of his presence is different. Effectively, the remembered becomes present as something that is not now but that was before. It is, therefore, a presence of the absent, the presence of what is not now, in the same way that perceived objects become present to me as current presence of the present.

But we have also said that remembering is a mode of consciousness, that is, a particular way in which consciousness reaches an object or in which an object appears to a consciousness and constitutes itself. We can call this mode of consciousness, "remembering consciousness". The object of the remembering consciousness is the remembered, in this case, my reading yesterday of Pessoa's *Book of Disquiet*. So what I remember is not my remembering consciousness, but its object, that is to say, I do not remember the remembering but the remembered. The importance that this checking has for ego analysis is immediately clear. If the ego is constituted by a framework of biographical and historical memories, it is transcendent of consciousness; as Sartre puts it, it is not the consciousness, it is something to which consciousness is directed in the remembering mode. It is an object of consciousness and not the consciousness itself. I am a doctor because I studied medicine and that is part of my ego, as is that I read Fernando Pessoa, or that I learnt how to play tennis when I was a child. We do not wish to mix these concepts and others obtained from different sources, as, for example, the distinctions made between implicit, explicit, episodic, and declarative memory. The fact that I play tennis today includes complex learnings and previous practices. However, in whichever way my history (the before-been) configures my ego and makes itself present in my life, it does not alter anything of that which we have mentioned.

To confuse ego with consciousness is, at the same time, to confuse any analysis that we perform in this field. My history, my story, constitutes my ego but not my consciousness. That is why we can exercise what we have denominated the "phenomenological attitude", that is, to put our ego in parentheses, to leave it in suspense and, in this way, to allow our consciousness to open up with the least bias possible to "the otherness" in the psychotherapeutic activity. To deduce from what we have said that the ego is not necessary, or that it is a device that we can live without, is to have read without attention what has been developed here. Suspension of the ego is only for the occasion of the psychotherapeutic encounter. If somebody practises it in other situations, besides, it is not a matter for our analysis here.

CHAPTER TEN

Psychotherapy based in "the other"

This subtitle is not original—it is taken from the psychotherapeutic approach of two notable English therapists, Caroline and David Brazier, which is grounded in Buddhist psychological principles and termed Other-Centred Therapy (Brazier, 2003). However, I must clarify that I will not specifically explore here the Braziers' thought and practice as, although what I write has found inspiration under that tradition, there are many other aspects to consider, especially philosophical and practical aspects that arise from sources other than Buddhism. It is common today for many aspects of psychotherapy to integrate among their techniques some of the traditional practices of Buddhism. This is the case, for instance, with mindfulness practices. However, caution is necessary when one searches for analogies and transcultural parallels due to the risk of trivialising (in a logical sense) and, with that, generating much confusion. In a book entitled *Gentle Bridges: Conversations with the Dalai Lama on the Sciences of Mind* (Hayward & Varela, 2001), co-edited by Francisco Varela, the eponymous "gentle bridges" are purportedly established between occidental science and the traditions of Buddhist wisdom. It is a provocative book, at times difficult to understand and, of course, for our purposes, important and revealing. But that importance has to do with something that the book does not pretend to aim at, or, perhaps more accurately, something contrary to its main objective. I refer to my appreciation, confirmed by the reading of that book, of the disjoint between, and irreducible character of, occidental empirical science and Buddhism (if we could even talk about "Buddhism" as a singular entity). I here use "science" in its more ordinary modern meaning, referring to empirical, positive, and experimental knowledge—for example, to the matrix of work in biology.

We have already mentioned the fundamental difference between these two approaches: occidental science is based, without exception, in the neutral third person, that is, it is always looking for the "thing" itself. Buddhism, by contrast, is grounded in the "first person", and particularly in the first person that is detached from the ego, the ego being the site of the concept of identity, of the "*mí mismo*" (myself) and the unrepeatable person we are, which gives a particular bias to our view of the "not-me". This ego detachment not only allows for less distortion in our access to material "things", but also to "the others" and the otherness in general. Despite these conceptions being substantively different, neither can be deemed "wrong". Effectively, and as we have mentioned repeatedly, the ego is the centre of our identity, of our history and of our personal projects. However, and as we also have mentioned, conscious states occur frequently in our daily life with no trace of ego, for example, as we focus deeply on reading a complex text, on a manual activity, or on a thought. The object of consciousness is, in these moments, not the ego, which, so to speak, remains "latent".

As we have insisted, the problem presents itself under the occidental view when trying to assimilate the consciousness into the ego. In our opinion, the fact that we can access a state in which it is evident that consciousness and the ego are not the same disproves the idea that consciousness necessarily has "personal contents". This admits many controversies but the point is that such controversies can be perfectly sterile. To talk about these matters is necessary so as not to lose sight of the experience and to agree that our material base and foundation is the way in which things occur to us. However, not everything is so different between occidental science and Buddhism. Indeed, occidental science's third-person approach is a part of its attempt to eradicate the investigator's "subjectivity", their bias and distorting view; ultimately, this is also about keeping the ego under control. This endeavour evidences occidental science's belief in the possibility of accessing a reality independent of what the individual investigator can access. There is in this a deep and ambiguous intuition: on the one hand, the idea that such access is possible and, on the other, an abiding doubt regarding our ability to see the otherness "just as it is". In extreme stances, this difficulty acquires the character of an impossibility and, as we have mentioned, it is even postulated that the "otherness" has no existence as such but is rather merely a construction based on the bias of our condition as knowing subjects. From there it seems that the entire methodological repertoire used to solve this *ab initio* contradiction is justified, that is, in the very origin of what is postulated and of which very little is spoken: what sense is there to postulate that there is *not* something like a reality "itself" and to then dedicate centuries to the attempt of apprehending it in its purity?

For its part, Buddhism sets out something similar: it is the ego (our identity) that impedes us from seeing "the otherness" just as it is (*rupa*). It is necessary then, as in occidental science, to elaborate a method that allows us to clear the consciousness of the ego. The difference is that Buddhism never calls into question the reality of "the otherness" as such, with its appearance, its glory, its measure, and its harmony. This would not be possible without the conviction and the experience of the possibility of suspending the ego. That is also the path of phenomenology ("to the things themselves") and that is why each of these methods, although with very different forms, have converged in this subject and are addressed in this text.

The psychotherapeutic setting based in "the other"

Essentially, psychotherapy is concerned with the space "between" subjectivities, one of which has tried, with varying levels of success, to put its ego in parentheses, which does not ordinarily occur in typical intersubjective interactions. This means that, for the therapist, it is *always* about "the other", about the "not-me". That is why he or she should be trained to suspend his or her ego, which, as we have seen, is not a simple, quick, or perfect process. Yet such training does not consist in the therapist "knowing him or herself", reaching his or her inner depths, or managing to solve his or her "intrapsychic" conflicts. It is just about being able to suspend the ego, to put it in parentheses, to leave it aside at the right moment, that is, in the psychotherapeutic frame. We psychotherapists are neither better nor wiser nor more developed persons than are our patients, and in no way can we manage without our ego in daily life. That is, the therapist's ego should not necessarily be "solved", "harmonious", "healthy", or similar—a state which is very hard to specify and settle without the intervention of a large number of prejudices and specific historical circumstances. It is not enough for there to be agreed criteria of "normality", formulated by groups of "experts" who represent diverse and complex interests, which, in my opinion, would not in any case be fulfilled by therapists in general as they are known as colleagues or friends. What we are saying is that *within* the psychotherapeutic frame, the ego of the therapist must be, as far as possible, disregarded.

The experience of the suspension of the ego, never absolute, is far from trivial as it allows us to access, although in an incomplete way, a state that is conscious but *impersonal.* That impersonality has nothing to do with indifference, scientific objectivity, or an external position regarding the therapeutic bond. As we have said, we therapists are not witnesses nor are we external to the system with a third-person attitude. Thus, the same question remains regarding the way in which intersubjectivity can be developed under these conditions. In effect, how can an intersubjectivity be established between one who is in a natural attitude and one who has suspended his or her identity, *mismidad* ("selfness") and personal history? That question is supported by an implicit premise: that the ego is synonymous with subjectivity and, therefore, if there are not two egos in an interaction there is no intersubjectivity. However, as we have already noted, subjectivity, *qualia,* and other similar expressions refer to *experiencing.* It is consciousness that first experiences our lives, while the ego is nothing other than those experiences throughout time, retained and retold within the biographical and cultural structure. It is not the ego that experiences, but consciousness. However, often in life, the ego guides experience, biases, self-refers, and models experience, and thus what is experienced (the tree I see, or the person with whom I live, or the world in general) remains subject to *fair* distortion. This point is crucial, so I will offer a clinical example.

S.O. is a forty-five year-old woman and she is separated. She does not have children. Among many other things, she experiences the following: when walking down the lane, and seeing a white object, such as a piece of paper, or a cigarette butt, she "sees it" as a consecrated wafer, and then "sees" that wafer elevating and introducing itself into her vagina. S.O. knows it is a piece of paper or a cigarette butt, however, she cannot help but "see" them as a consecrated wafer. She also knows these do not elevate and that they do not enter her vagina. However, I insist, she sees it. We have named this phenomenon a "pseudo illusion", like the illusion by which I see a "cockroach" in a corner of the kitchen: I come closer, and I see it is a black grape. The illusion appears when I correct it; before that point I believe I am perceiving correctly. In the case of S.O. those two times do not exist separately, but the right and the wrong perception occur simultaneously or, if preferred, in parallel. With great anguish and disgust toward herself, S.O. must retrace the path and walk again by the same spot she saw the white object, but without looking at it. This is very difficult for her and she doubts if she effectively did not look at it, which is why she must repeat this many times until she is sure. This situation makes walking one block take many hours.

I have never experienced anything similar, nor do I have a vagina, nor am I religious, nor have I experienced pseudo illusions. What I am experiencing now is what S.O. (that person, that subjectivity, that other) is telling me and all the emotions that overwhelm her. Nothing of this has to do with my personal history, but I "empathise" without difficulty with her and her experiences. I am conscious of her story, of her emotions, and her tortured suffering. When talking about consciousness, we emphasised that it is not always the same, that is, consciousness may be perceptive, emotional, imaginary, remembering, etc. There are different means by which we can reach intentional objects. In the mentioned example, I understand S.O. in a primary way: there is no interference by my age, my sex, my history, in short, my ego. I can, then, proceed to "extension": when did the event she is recounting occur? What does "consecrated wafer" mean to her? Is she religious, does she receive communion, does she share with somebody her suffering, does she hide it? The extension proceeds in this manner. Could we affirm, given this extension, that there has not been intersubjectivity and that the patient has been "alone"?

Evidently, during the process, thoughts, memories, and a variety of knowledge come to me. For example, I can rush to some reasonable conjectures, as the following: S.O. does not observe that the host in her vagina is a sexual act between God (Christ's body) and a human, mortal woman. That is, she wants to be the Virgin and have God's son in her womb. But I could also think that she simply wants to have the child she never had, and that she blames the God she believes in, so that she humiliates him by introducing him into her vagina. We could go on.

Inconveniently, those conjectures are to do with my ego, with theories or learnt styles of understanding that have to do with my personal history. But if I allow an extension while simultaneously rejecting all rushed interpretations, including a diagnosis of obsessive-compulsive disorder (OCD), the patient's own version of her experience will appear and my consciousness will access what in actuality torments her. This takes time, and is no trivial feat.

There is no doubt at all that the reader has already performed his or her own interpretations and imposed his or her own narratives regarding S.O., even though the reader does not know the patient, does not know how she is physically, does not know her language, her cognitive abilities, her cultural level, or her life story. It is tempting to offer a further account of S.O.'s condition following therapy, but suffice to say she never recovered from her sufferings in a meaningful way, despite taking the right psychotropic drugs, and working in a "specific" psychotherapeutic model for two years. I also imagine that the reader will wonder if, had he or she performed the therapy, the result would have been otherwise. It is possible.

CHAPTER ELEVEN

"The other" in psychotherapy

The experience of leaving the ego in parentheses can be frightening, as it is akin to eliminating all sense of supports that permanently govern us. When doing psychotherapy, nobody is Peter, nor a "great therapist", nor a "great academic", nor a "wise person": the therapist is not even him or herself. The therapist is, so to speak, "nobody". Not an "ego" capable of neutrality, but the most basic mode of consciousness, which, we insist, is impersonal. We emphasise this point as it is the cornerstone of what we have said thus far and it is tremendously counter-intuitive. But, on the other hand, this suspension of the ego can offer a state of pure serenity, as the impersonal consciousness allows us to open up, in a privileged way, to the panorama offered by the world ("the otherness" and "the other").

How can we establish intersubjectivity in these conditions of subjective asymmetry? It is clear that the patient, so to speak, is in a "natural attitude", they are not a phenomenologist nor have they training in meditation. Therefore, they speak and behave from the ego. This is how things should be, furthermore, because this is how our daily life is.

The first thing that stands out is that the spontaneous patient (and not the one who is looking to meet a requirement to be a therapist themselves), that is, the one who seeks help because their suffering is in some sense extreme, painful, or disabling, has very much to tell: of what they experience, of their life, of their job, of their love bonds, etc. In other words, they need to speak of *themselves*, that is, from their ego. It is natural: the ego is *all* that we can talk about. Ego is a syntax, a tale, a network story and, like all syntax and all language, it is formed by the articulation of parts or moments in a temporal sequence (diachrony) and in a structural articulation (synchrony).

The patient is talking about him or herself. But, what is it to speak about "one's" self? To talk about *my* self, paradoxically, is to talk in unison about "the otherness" and "the others" from the bias of my own identity. The person feels anguish *about something*, is sad *about something*, is angry *with somebody*, feels despised *by somebody or by many*, feels pain in *his or her head*, does not get along with *her husband*, is doing poorly *at school*, feels unfairly criticised *by her boss*, feels depressed on *cloudy days*, just lost *his house*, has conflict with *her teenage children*, just received a diagnosis of *colon cancer*, is terrified of *earthquakes*, failed in the *exit exam*, as a child was abused by *her stepfather*, ejaculates prematurely when he has sexual intercourse with *his partner*, cannot concentrate on *reading*, cannot make sense of *the day*, finds it difficult to make decisions *in her job*, etc. It is evident that all that is in italics is "other", including the body in its being nature, as we will shortly see.

According to what we have said up to now, we should suppose that all that "other" is disfigured by the force of the patient's ego, via the bias we have termed *rupa*. However, that supposition can lead us to believe that our role is to make the patient see things just as they are, given that we, under this training, have overcome the *rupa* state to perceive things clearly and truthfully. Yet this is far from the point of psychotherapy: we, as therapists, have some control over our own ego, but that does not give us access to "how things are", in fact, for another. We do not know how her boss behaves because we do not have the boss before us nor do we know him. All we have is the way in which the patient refers to them. An apparent contradiction thus appears: how can we help a patient break with the self-reference of *rupa* if there is nothing before us, such as her boss, "just the way he is"? It is easy to confuse the phenomenological attitude with the state of an absolute and omniscient "observer". This apparent confusion can lead to the temptation of hermeneutics—in the sense of comprehensive interpretation—that is rushed and theoretically biased.

What is evident is that many varied persons and situations appear as told by the patient. We can then ask the patient to *extend to us* those others and to tell us more of, for instance, that boss of whom she is afraid: what does he look like, how does he speak, how does he dress, how does he gesticulate aggressively, with whom does he behave in this way? It is about, as Caroline Brazier puts it, "seeing" with the patient's eyes. Something surprising thus appears: the deformation of *rupa* is not an absolute state, it is not a hallucinatory phenomenon, it is not a pure creation or construction of the patient's ego, but rather a *covering*, in that the other, so to speak, remains hidden and veiled by the patient's self-reference while, *at the same time*, remaining implicit. The expansion, then, makes many aspects of the other apparent for the patient that he had perceived, but that had remained unnoticed. In this sense, the Greek word *aletheia* used to express "the truth" demonstrates its fruitfulness: it is about neutralizing (denoted by the *a*-prefix) "the forgetting" (*lethe*), that is, it is about remembering, about rescuing what is already known but that, in everyday life, has remained hidden.

It is important to emphasise that what we are expressing is not a technique, but simply the product of seeing the other immersed in his or her world that, instead of being an *internal* world, is a world "of others", that is, *external*. This should no longer surprise us: all that consciousness refers to is "external" to it, is "transcendent" to it. That is why ego is "transcendent", as it is not "inside" consciousness, but as much outside of consciousness as any other intentional object.

What we intend is that the patient, with our help, is able to see implicit aspects of others and situations, aspects he or she knows, but that are obscured by self-reference. However, our "help" can, with great ease, be conditioned by our expertise and especially by our theoretical constructions. This means that, for example, we can believe that in offering a clinical diagnosis, as of OCD for S.O., we are getting to know her or that we already know about her in some sense. We should be able to note whether the intersubjective space appears intertwined with theories and generalisations independent of the person with whom we are presented. While not the subject of this essay, we have written in many places (and have mentioned here) the taxonomic and clinical inconsistencies of the *Diagnostic and Statistical Manual of Mental Disorders* (Ojeda, 1993). Yet, given the recent fifth edition of the manual (American Psychiatric Association, 2013), we cannot help but underline that, instead of practising some level of reflection and self-criticism, the DSM insists on repeating the same prejudices and mistakes, thinking that over 300 "mental disorders" can be "assigned" to those who seek psychological help, without noting that, in large part, it is a capricious and illogical list of prejudices and interests, and not just clinical but also social, economic, and anthropological.

CHAPTER TWELVE

The orientation of change in psychotherapy

The therapist does not have to know where the patient will orient his or her change, nor how the patient will rebuild the story about him or herself. That is, the therapist does not know how the patient will assemble what is revealed during the psychotherapeutic process, nor the way in which the patient will take into account the elements of his or her experience that were once veiled and that are now, at some level, exposed. The therapist neither has the power to assemble the story of the other (the patient's ego) as he or she likes nor capriciously.

When aspects, perspectives, and elements that had previously been hidden come to light, the patient, in a spontaneous way, tends to take them into account and thereby change his or her story, as the reference of the world *is no longer just him or her as ego.* Usually, the patient has been talking of others, but inadvertently doing so *through* himself. So to speak, the flow of existence now takes a different course, whereby others are a linked part but also autonomous, whereby the world in general is also a part but infinitely extensive and, fundamentally, in which the patient, being a mere part, does not govern very much. The patient is not even the owner of the realisation of the project of their life, which usually takes unpredictable courses, and they have even less control over the script that their body develops in an autonomous way. It is common to feel the relief that patients experience upon accepting "the otherness" as a reality that is not there *just* for them but *with* them, that does not depend *just* on them and of which the patient should not *necessarily* take charge in an isolated and lonely way. But, the anguish the patient feels when faced with the unanchored nature of existence is also evident and palpable. As we have already mentioned: who can predict the course that each individual's life takes? The fact that everything changes constantly does not depend on the will of each person, but instead occurs in spontaneous ways. This is what the Buddha called "impermanency".

What does the therapist do in order for the described insight to bloom? The answer to this question can be developed extensively, but maybe it would be most helpful to offer the fundamental matter in a few lines, before trying to provide further development. It seems that the first thing a therapist does is to move out of the way; the second is that he or she helps to put words to the patient's world, to emphasise the nodes and what is implicit in the stories the patient tells in an automatic and self-referential way; the third is that he or she believes in the patient, that is, he or she exiles suspicion as a working method.

Moving out of the way

It is not easy for the therapist to move out of the way of the patient's progress. We have developed this concept as the "phenomenological attitude", "putting the ego in parentheses", and similar expressions. In saying "out of the way" we are supposing that there are two parts in the process and we tend to think that one of them is the therapist and the other is the patient. It is evident that there is a "between" in that relationship, but at this moment we are referring to the "between" of the patient and *the other* to him, *the other* of which the therapist is just a tiny part. If the patient affirms that his father was authoritarian, instead of standing "between" the patient and his father, we stand next to him. From the laterality, we can see that what the patient is saying is not just that he was authoritarian, but also a working man, with a remarkable "gift" of authority, and that he used to face problems with not much faltering and solved them efficiently. The patient sees all that and shows it, but emphasises what affected *him* concerning the dominant attitude of his father at the moments that authoritarianism was *regarding* him.

When asking him to "show us" his father, we are asking him to refer to his father as himself. We are not asking how *he* felt, but how *his* father was. Patients know many of those meanings for others. It is surprising that, on occasion, patients start narrating their lives from the perspective of their grandparents, parents, siblings, political or economic situation, the era, etc. They do so as if watching a movie or reading a novel for the first time. I want to say in this regard that in the telling there is less self-reference and more "novelty", not just for the therapist but also for the patient himself. It is indeed this "novelty" that allows patients to read their lives from other angles and, especially, from the presence of the other as such. Nothing of this has to do with the therapist, whose role is, so to speak, to transform the soliloquy into a dialogue, taking the place of "another".

The words

What does the therapist say? Maybe this is the most subtle point in a therapeutic relationship. It can be useful to start from what the therapist does not say. They do not speak of themselves, but *from* what the patient has said, including all the expressive elements of the interaction; that is, the therapist speaks from "the other". The therapist has better practice in doing so than does the patient, but not much more than that. That is, the encounter, progressively, becomes symmetrical, with first the therapist and then the patient becoming open to the not-me world. For the therapist, the "not-me" is the patient and his world. Often we feel inclined to explain to the patient what occurs in their meaningful interactions with others or to "interpret", that is, to add coherences that the narrated facts suggest. It would be conceited to emphasise that this should not happen.

M.U., upon arriving home, sees her husband H.S. sitting and drained on the couch watching TV. He has in his hands the afternoon newspaper and on the coffee table is a pair of cans of beer. She says hello to him and he answers with a monosyllable, not paying greater attention. This causes in her a mixture of anger, sadness, and disdain.

From this description (a lot more extensive in reality) the therapist can follow various paths. One of them is to incite the patient to delve into the anger, the sadness, and the disdain she is feeling. Yet, also, the therapist can look further than that to which the patient refers, than what provokes those feelings. The therapist can ask: did your husband seem tired? What is his job? What is his schedule? She has introduced a man who seems tired and apathetic *regarding her* and what it causes in *her*. Naturally, it is not necessary to explain to her that she is not the centre of her husband's life, nor is it the case that everything he does has to do with her. That, at the right time, will come about on its own. What we are trying to achieve is for the patient to tell us what she knows: her husband's activities and the demands he is under.

H.S. is an engineer in a telecommunications enterprise, where he works very much and under great pressure. M.U. knows that they are paying off a very expensive mortgage loan (payment in which she herself cannot cooperate) as they purchased an expensive house by mutual agreement. Frequently, H.S. does not have the time nor the energy to talk with her and listen to her, especially on subjects related to the thesis she is pursuing at the university to obtain her PhD (a burdensome endeavour which also means a drain on the family budget). When he listens to her it is evident that he is expending great effort. They have two little children (five and seven years old) who demand plenty of attention. He rarely comes home in time to see them before they are asleep, but he takes them every morning to school and, on weekends, he usually goes out with them to some park, or takes them to the tennis club, or rides a bicycle with them along a bicycle lane near where they live. M.U. normally uses these periods when they are not at home to advance her thesis and obtain the materials she needs from the online library of the university.

At the beginning of therapy, it is often difficult for patients to talk about others. When they do so, it tends to be with regards to themselves, as they consider that psychotherapy is about "a space for me", or some similar sentiment, often expressed in the early sessions. However, gradually, the stories concerning significant others become more and more comprehensive. After recounting the above, for instance, a subtle change occurs in the patient M.U.: the episode that affected her so deeply in the early session has gradually faded to the extent that its context has been extended.

The therapist can remain quiet for long moments. What that silence produces is a type of triangulation: the patient speaks to the therapist about other persons and situations and not of him or herself.

It is possible that, as the therapy advances, the therapist and patient generate a wide, shared world that is basically *other*, in a different way, for both. It is in this moment that the therapist can join, separate,

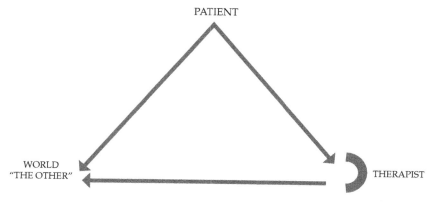

Figure 3. Therapeutic triangulation.

synthesise, and project the ingredients of this world, being cautious not to include any contents that have not been expressed by the patient.

The elimination of suspicion

"Suspicion" has a legal connotation. People are suspicious to the extent that somebody supposes they have done something criminal and, naturally, the suspect hides. The suspicious are examined. When suspecting, we are suspicious of the other and we develop the attitude of an inquisitor or, not rarely, a detective. I protest frequently when psychiatrists use the phrase "to interrogate the patient" because of precisely these connotations. Suspicion is the opposite of faith in the other.

Despite the fact that the above sounds obvious, we must address, from it, something much less evident, which has multiple ramifications for psychotherapy. I mean the "invisible", which does not appear in the first instance, but which instead underlies. This has a long history in occidental thought, of which psychotherapy is in fact a consequence. Let us remember, although superficially, that the expression "school of suspicion" was coined by the French philosopher Paul Ricoeur in 1965. He referred to three thinkers of the nineteenth century who, in his opinion, unmasked the falseness hidden under the erudite values of rationality and truth: Marx, Nietzsche, and Freud. The idea of unmasking carries with it an undeniable hint of denunciation. That is, a way of forcing the hooded other to show their true face. Thus, Marx unmasks ideology as false or inverted consciousness; Nietzsche questions false values; Freud lays bare the customs of unconscious impulses. "A new problem has been born", says Ricoeur, "consciousness as a *lie*" (Ricoeur, 1975, p. 5). This way of seeing the problem cannot be dismantled by the stroke of a pen. However, when using categories of ordinary language, in which, for example, "truth" and "lie" are opposed, we can find ourselves radicalising a discussion that admits many perspectives and nuances. The ideas of "bringing to light", "clarity and distinction", "revealing", "laying bare", along with many other visual metaphors have, in occidental thought, great influence and are primary in practically all psychotherapeutic models. It is enough to remember that *theorein* in Greek means "to look carefully". Before the enlightened beginning (clear and evident), we are asleep or blind. We need to look, to draw back the veil that covers what is there in order to make it present, to bring it to light, and to rescue it from forgetting. However, we are not necessarily dealing here with an ethical subject: the lie *requires* that the truth be known, and for that it will always be *deliberately false*. I believe in the invisible, while the spotlight is somewhere else. As we have mentioned, perhaps the more moving occidental concept of truth is expressed in the Greek word *aletheia*, which means to suppress forgetting (*lethe*) or, if you will, to remember. To remember what we have always known, but that has been hidden from our sight.

Claude Lévi-Strauss (Lévi-Strauss, 1974) considered that Freudianism, geology, and Marxism realised a similar insight, given that they each postulated that understanding consists in reducing one kind of reality to another, as the real sense of the individual, social, and geological processes is never in view. To make the processes evident we must proceed from the surface (the evident) to the depth (the hidden). Independently of these spatial concepts of "surface" and "depth", this idea clearly concerns the evident and the veiled. In psychotherapy there is no room for ethical radicalisation: patients are not *liars*, but, for diverse reasons, they do not see what they know. Among these reasons it seems to us that *rupa*, the self-covering of the world, is one, and not the least important.

As we know, Heidegger put forth wide developments regarding the "truth" in the original Greek sense already mentioned. We have dedicated detailed analysis to Heidegger in other writings, so we will not repeat here what is written elsewhere (Ojeda, 2006). It is enough to mention that this philosopher maintains a beautiful ambiguity in this field: humans (to him we, humans, are *Dasein*, that is, beings open to his being, although the chosen expression does not mean this in ordinary German) are in the truth and in the non-truth at the same time. How does this happen? Through re-covering what has already been and has always been discovered. Why "re-cover" (in the sense of veiling, clouding, covering, etc.) the uncovered? Ultimately, due to the anguish and the suffering elicited in us before the finiteness that shakes us while we live. Heidegger calls the "covering" process "fall" (Verfallen).

The persons who ask for help generally present some form of anguish. In saying "form" maybe we express ourselves inadequately. What we want to say is that the anguish, which is ultimately universal, usually comes in diverse clothing. When Heidegger formulates his "being-towards-death", he does so using an entangled language. However, there are many entangled postulates that have not enjoyed any of being-towards-death's historical fortune. Heidegger's case is different, because, despite his linguistic affectation and his implicit philosophical battles, he expresses something that anybody can acknowledge as an authentic and truthful experience. Briefly, Heidegger says we do not choose to live but yet we find ourselves living and know that, sooner rather than later, our final destiny (in the short-term) is to stop living. To go from existent (beings open to being) to absolute nothingness is incomprehensible and, to a large extent, absurd. It is absurd because it causes suffering without allowing for understanding of purpose, rendering us blindly subdued as conscious beings to such destiny.

Yet the issue is not the fact of the end of living, of dying, but rather the fact of having to exist *as you live* with that certainty. The uncertainty that mounts on that one and only certainty is when and how it will occur in the end. Let us remember that in Descartes, certainty was of existence as an experience. Now Heidegger makes a curious Copernican somersault: *the certainty of existing does not occur if it is not mounted on the certainty of ceasing to exist.* I am warned that these approaches seem somewhat dramatic and, for many, exaggerated. Indeed, it seems that way on a first encounter. But as we gain understanding of what produces suffering in those who are in psychotherapy, we can confirm that a great part is related to that "being-towards-death".

There is not, therefore, a lying consciousness, but only an anaesthetised consciousness, a consciousness that has huge difficulties in accepting what it already knows. Each time we ask about the mind, we know, beforehand, that we cannot avoid asking ourselves about consciousness and, we also know, we will never have a satisfactory answer. The mystery is not solved via definitions or conventional agreements. We can reflect widely and intensely on our consciousness, but we never find it as something *in there* or, in the style of archaeology, some entity we could dig up as "something". In the same way, the "internal" contents of persons seem to be something that we could uncover, as when we open a gift box and we find in there "things". Is it not this that psychotherapy usually offers? Do not patients think that, through psychotherapy, they will get to know themselves, that they will gain clarity about what they really are? It is not easy to convey the point that what they will find is *not-me* and nothing internal to consciousness.

CHAPTER THIRTEEN

Dualism

It seems that overcoming dualism was a manifestation of the evolved thought of both theoretical psychotherapists and philosophers. However, "I am my body" is an extraordinarily fragile postulate (and a fashion). Precisely the most heart-rending revelation regarding human beings is that which tells us the contrary, which tells us that the I (ego), *my* personal story and its script, is, to a large extent, independent of the body. The body, in a certain way, defines us and affects us but, surprisingly, my project of personal life is indifferent to my body. "Your neurons could not care less who you are", said Daniel Dennett (2008), hitting the target this time, in my opinion. The body has an independent project and does not consult us in that pursuit. Growing old or getting sick is enough for us to realise that the body has not taken into consideration anything of our life project, of our desires and our responsibilities. What relationship is there between a degenerative sickness (such as multiple sclerosis) and the ego; what does the ego have to do with a myocardial infarction? Does the ego have anything to say about it? This is why it is so difficult to hold onto the realisation of unavoidable death. In our opinion, the tension between the ego and the body is a source of great suffering in people. Although not seen exactly like that, we have been surprised to find in clinical practice that this tension is implicit and is the founding of a great quantity of human suffering. This is why we have an interest in wisdom traditions that are very different from ours, such as Buddhism, for which this tension is explicit and developed as an essential part of its practices and conceptions of human life.

Nature as "otherness": first step of a dualist outline

We human beings do not just experience the "not-me" intersubjectively, but also as a generic "otherness". This is how it occurs with respect to *nature,* which is an aspect of what we are but also of *what we are not* and what confronts us in the world in the midst of which we live. The mountain range, the air, and the partridges are natural, but also, in a certain sense, we are natural too. This ontic community (community of "things") is appreciated when we are hit by a hard and heavy object, similarly if a rock is detached from a hillside, or a piece of Caesar's statue falls due to an earthquake's pounding. In such cases we discover the naturalness of all these objects, but also the naturalness of our own body. Indeed, there is a constituent aspect of our existence that, like carbon, is in the earth, but is also a part, and a legitimate part, of what we are. We refer to the body considered as *Körper,* that is, as material and extensive body. Here it is not about the expressive, aesthetic, or physiognomic (*Leib*) body, nor the theoretical body (*Bíos*), but the "living thing" we are. This "living thing", no matter how it is usually hidden and silenced as such a thing, when it appears to us it does so as an experience and not as a speculative category. That experience is the experience of a failure, of a fault, of a "break-up", of a script that separates us from the one we supposed we had to ourselves. Our stomach only appears when we are nauseous or in pain. Before that, it is mute. That "failure" (in an almost geological sense) defines, dissociates, and underscores, at that moment, a difference between the sense parameters that define us as the person we are and the nature we also are.

Human beings organise their existence as identity, that is, according to a personal history and project, full of acts that provide for them a non-transferrable biographical unit (ego). To be a doctor, a writer, or public servant; to be a father or a mother of one's children; to be a friend, a master, or a disciple; to be a child of one's parents; to be a sister or brother; to belong to a country; to speak a natively determined language; to have a proper name, allow us to escape seriality. This means that, being such a being as I am, the network formed by my social, familial, and professional bonds is unique to me and nobody can occupy the same intersection determined by those bonds. It is at this level that the sense of the individual human life (the self and biography) flows, providing for each person an unrepeatable and familiar character, constituting the plexus of significances (stories) of the mentioned identity.

Yet nature, so to speak, moves in cycles and unavoidable transformations which, despite not being available for us, are nevertheless always mute and express also part of what we are. This we always already know: to be born, to grow old, to get ill, and to die are part of the natural flow.

In what we term "panic attacks" we attend to a *tragedy* (in the original Greek sense of that word), to a tear and, at the same time, to a revelation. The person realises that something is occurring within their body that indicates an imminent dissolution: tachycardia, dyspnoea, the sensation of loss of consciousness—unequivocal signs for them that the nature which they properly are has entered a cycle of disease and death. But this property, this aspect of what we are, is, at the same time and paradoxically, an alienation (and there is the revelation): alienation regarding the personal project and, therefore, the lack of purpose and absurdity of life. This dissociation happens in a sudden and uncontrollable way. Yet, relentlessly, the "failure", that "failure" that I now experience, makes my beliefs, my disputes, my pretensions, and my small desires irrelevant, with the exception of the reality of death that reminds me that I too am part of nature and, consequently, I cannot escape from it. That "failure", whether insinuated, symbolised, or frank, is the crack from which appears what we call anguish: anguish before nature that, in an unavoidable sense, we also are, but that, nevertheless, is not all that we are. If that tension, that definition, and that break-up did not exist, what sense would there be in the agony, the fight for the persistence of an aspect of the being that I am, and that I feel to be the more authentically mine as it is the plexus of significances that has presided over my human life?

However, nature also threatens us in other ways. In what we call specific phobias, the fear of nature is no longer directed at the individual's own body, but rather at animals, catastrophes, darkness, storms, etc. The same occurs in relation to technology that subdues man with powerful machines and enormous constructions liable to suffer flaws, errors, and irregularities that can, in an absurd way, harm or annihilate the project of life that makes sense of us. It is not possible to make a "pact" with all these situations: once triggered, the natural mechanics are blind, powerful, and ruthless to us. What surprises us, and in a certain sense is paradoxical, is that which has already been mentioned many times: that same nature is also an aspect of what we are as existent humans. In this there is no possible intersubjectivity, given that the nature we are, and in which we are, lacks subjectivity, that is, this nature's aspect is not an "other" like me, which is the only situation in which intersubjectivity is possible.

Nature as "the other": second step of a dualist outline

However, not all threats appear from nature as otherness in its non-subjective fates, laws, and transformations, but also from "the" other, that is, otherness realised in persons like me. As we have mentioned before, the sense that presides over the development of an individual's life considers, from the start, the presence of other persons with which, in diverse ways, we establish familial, social, and professional bonds (second person). Unlike abstract humanity, these factual bonds give each individual their "place", their space of belonging and identity by which being the person I am acquires not just its features, but also its rights and non-transferrable obligations. To respect, to love, to value "certain" others, and to be respected, loved, and valued by them in turn is not something dispensable or adjectival: it is essential for the development of the possibilities of each one of us. Failure before the others who we care about and who define us does not relate with the above-discussed nature that simultaneously enables and limits, with that dimension that gives rise to both our birth and death, but with the necessary ingredient of the meaning of human life, always already "with others". In what context, if not this, can uniquely human experiences be understood, such as embarrassment, blame, envy, humiliation, etc.? None of these feelings could exist without "the" other in the second person. It is the experience of any psychotherapist that these kinds of states, frequently, cause great subjective suffering. Indeed, it constitutes one of the main reasons for consultation in our job. For example, embarrassment is only possible under the gaze of the other, by their witnessing. Among the daily acts of any person, there are many that are conducted in solitude and are, so to speak, neutral, yet with the simple look of the other and without the other substantively affecting the act, it is transformed into something shameful. Thus, the deciding component in this case is not the act itself, but the act's being before the other's gaze. In the case of guilt, it is about the fact of owing something to these others, of not having lived up to what they deserve and what thereby, in many aspects, defines my self-perception. For its part, envy is about something I do not have, which I lack and which I think the other has that dignifies him or her. It is also the other who actively reduces me in my human condition when he or she humiliates me. All these feelings are complex but, in offering this sketch, what I want to emphasise is that in all cases it is the other that is definitional. That is, the other who is close, loved, or valued, who is "significant" to us—who is the second person—rather than any other not thus related to us, is also a source to us of uncertainty and fear. In the so-called social and sexual phobias, the fear appears before a person or group of persons with whom the subject has a significant bond in situations in which a personal and non-transferrable behaviour is expected from the subject, that is, situations in which the subject is specified and cannot be anonymous. Who, if not me, is presenting at this conference? Who, if not me, is friends with that person who walks along the sidewalk across the street? If the others in such cases and in many senses define me and I care about them, then that one, which I indicate when I say "me", who is in front of those others, must take charge: charge of being *myself.*

Here there is no reference to death. In the road of taking charge, there is no longer the anguish before the finiteness imposed on me, but another form we could call "interpersonal" or "egoic anguish", given that it makes explicit the faint and fragile mask of all the considerations about myself, it makes me recognise the dependence that being myself has on the other and how, frequently, I regard myself through the eyes of that other. That is why my hand shakes when signing, why I forget what I am saying, why I do not know what to say in that casual meeting with a friend on the street, why I blush when realizing that the attention of the customers has stopped on me, why my sexual answer is blocked or hurried before the desired partner. From this grounding, the phobic mechanism parasitises the structure, it fixes it, and takes charge of repeating the above.

However, while the other looks at me, I too can look at him or her. In accordance with Sartre, here we find the dialectics of the liberties, the fight, and the conflict. In the presence of the other, there are at least two possible attitudes: either we affirm ourselves as subjects and in doing so appropriate the other's freedom and treat their being as an object (using it as a tool), or we try to capture the other in their freedom, in their being a subject themselves, but in doing so running the risk of losing our own liberty and becoming mere objects to that other. This is why Sartre affirms that, in either attitude, the relationship between subjectivities will always be *troubled* and will fundamentally be a fight between liberties. This leads to his pessimistic conclusion, that "hell is other people". It is easy not to share this affirmation, but it would be blind not to acknowledge the daily unrest that arises among persons that are bonded closely together. Dramatists know this well: dramatic conflict always arises from the closest bonds.

Love

Maybe this is this second form of anguish (ego anguish) which allows us to enter a field that transcends the matter of the Heideggerian finiteness and that forces us to acknowledge that "the other" is an essential part of my life, that I care for, that demands me, that gives to me, that torments me, that inspires hope in me, that disappoints me, that angers me, and that, as we say, anguishes me in a pre-eminent way.

If we polish this concept a little, it is possible to perceive that the list is a relevant part of what we call "intersubjectivity" and that, in the midst of these vicissitudes, is what we also call, with certain sheepishness, "love" or its privative states (heartbreak, loneliness, abandonment, anger, disdain, etc.). It is curious that, by contrast to priests, ministers, and other religious guides, psychotherapists rarely mention the word "love". Instead, we talk about an "affective bond" or some similar expression. It is clear that "love" is not a technical term. Is it worth investigating and explicating the phenomenon we call "love" in ordinary life (which is common to everyone) and that, along with being for the death of Heidegger, is the phenomenon that produces a very important part of human suffering? Is not the absent, painful, broken, or deceased love one of the main subjects that leads a person to ask for psychotherapeutic help? We will not answer this question here, as there is nothing more distant from our purpose than the transformation of this brief book into a treatise. We simply suggest it as a conversation.

EPILOGUE

A few days before finishing this text I concluded my reading of the novel *Contigo en la Distancia* ("With You in the Distance"), by Carla Guelfenbein (2015). The author was born in Chile and received, with this work, the Alfaguara Novel Prize in 2015. A colleague, a literature lover, asked me if the novel was "good", given that the "literary critics" had been rather negative. I thought of answering "yes", then "no", and, finally, "yes and no". This episode clarified for me that, for a literary work, as for the lives of persons, this kind of global judgement is not possible. The novel has memorable and inspiring paragraphs, and others that are trivial and flat; it has convincing sections, and others that are unlikely; some passages are spontaneous, others seem assembled and gummed-up. The story, at times, has the character of the impossible and, at others, of situations known by everybody. It is a novel of love and non-love, of death and negation of death, of frivolity and transcendence.

Up to that moment I could not have imagined that this novel would be part of the Epilogue of this small work about subjectivity and psychotherapy. What happened was rather simple. We, persons, are also a certain kind of story, in which historical and biographical (ego) ingredients are many and composed of textures irreducible to language.

This last point was the one that generated this connection between psychotherapy and literature. The human experience is evident, but at the same time ineffable, that is, impossible to say. One regularly hears and reads that "language creates realities", that "we are in language", that "we are language" and similar expressions. It is possible that this is sometimes the case, but the greater part of the human experience is independent of words. Saint Augustine noted that all persons know what time is until they try to explain it. The same occurs also for love, anguish, pleasure, pain, perplexity, disappointment, nostalgia, humiliation, shyness, fascination, understanding, and many other ordinary phenomena in human experience without which a human psyche would not be imaginable as such. It is possible that descriptions help to specify and give shape to these phenomena, but they do not in any way constitute *definitions.* I cannot define shyness as I do parallels in Euclidean geometry, because human experience is not axiomatic. Maybe this is the greatest difficulty of empirical research in this field: research in the third person *must* define, as it cannot operate with the vague, the ambiguous, the diffuse, the mysterious, or the ineffable.

It is not, then, about defining. The point we have tried to make here is that words help to unveil, to make evident what we already know but that is blurry, to describe the experienced complex, to know all that should first *be there.* The experience of the patient S.O., which we noted within the text, is prior to all our descriptive attempts and also her own. We first live, then we speak, and intersubjectivity, as we have addressed it in this text, is experienced from beginning to end and not primarily through language. From this, we can naturally deduce that sense and meaning are not linguistic phenomena in the first instance. There are 7,000 human languages, and in all of them we can express the experience which, in Spanish, we indicate with the sound and graphology *perro* ("dog"), but this is expressed with different sounds and graphology in different languages. The sounds *perro, dog* and *Hund* are not those that make the dog, but the dog itself experienced by our consciousness.

We have also said that intersubjectivity precedes language and, among other experiences, has to do with the vision of an "other like me" who also sees me "as another like him or her". This does not occur in this way because it is said or not said as such: it just occurs. I believe that literature is a gifted attempt to say something of what occurs to us, but (and this is what is wonderful about it) it is an attempt that is always failed and incomplete. In the same way, in reality, psychotherapy never arrives at a determinate result, much less a prior determined result. Psychotherapy cannot, in a strict sense, "be completed" and, nevertheless, it ends. This occurs at some moment, independently of what the therapist believes. Maybe it is so difficult to end a novel for the same reason, because there is no reason for it to have an end. However, in reality, they always end somehow.

REFERENCES

American Psychiatric Association. (2013). *Diagnostic and Statistical Manual of Mental Disorders,* fifth edition. Arlington, VA: American Psychiatric Publishing.

Brazier, C. (2003). *Buddhist Psychology: Liberate your mind, embrace life.* Berkeley: Ulysses.

Chardin, T. (1967). *El Grupo Zoológico Humano* [The Human Zoological Group]. Madrid: Taurus.

Dennett, D. (1991). *Consciousness Explained.* New York: Little, Brown.

Dennett, D. (2008). "Las células no saben quién eres, ni les importa": entrevista con Daniel Dennett ["Cells do not know who you are, and they don't care": interview with Daniel Dennett]. *Rev GPU* 4 (4): 411–415.

Depraz, N., Varela, F., & Vermersch, P. (2003). *On Becoming Aware: a Pragmatics of Experiencing.* Amsterdam: John Benjamins.

Descartes, R. (1980). *Meditaciones Metafísicas* [Meditations on First Philosophy]. Madrid: Espasa-Calpe.

Guelfenbein, C. (2015). *Contigo en la Distancia* [With You in the Distance]. Santiago: Alfaguara.

Hayward, J., & Varela, F. (Eds.) (2001). *Gentle Bridges: Conversations with the Dalai Lama on the Sciences of Mind.* Boston & London: Shambhala.

Hegel, G. H. F. (1966). *Fenomenología del Espíritu* [Phenomenology of Spirit]. Mexico: Fondo de Cultura Económica.

103

Heidegger, M. (1997). *Ser y Tiempo* [Being and Time]. Santiago: Universitaria.

Husserl, E. (1979). *Meditationes Cartesianas* [Cartesian Meditations]. Madrid: Paulinas.

Husserl, E. (1980). *Experiencia y Juicio* [Experience and Judgement]. Mexico: Universidad Autónoma de México.

Husserl, E. (1986). *Ideas relativas a una fenomenología pura y una filosofía fenomenológica* [Ideas Related to a Pure Phenomenology and a Phenomenological Philosophy]. Mexico: Fondo de Cultura Económica.

Husserl, E. (1998). *Invitación a la Fenomenología* [Invitation to Phenomenology]. Barcelona: Paidós.

Krauss, N. (2002). *Man Walks into a Room*. New York: Doubleday [reprinted London: Penguin, 2007].

Lacan, J. (2003). *El seminario de Jacques Lacan (The Seminar of Jacques Lacan). Libro 8, La transferencia 1960–1961*. Buenos Aires: Paidós.

Leibniz, G. (1980). *Monadología* [The Monadology]. Buenos Aires: Aguilar.

Lévi-Strauss, C. (1974). *Antropología Estructural* [Structural Anthropology]. Barcelona: Paidos.

Maturana, A., & Varela, F. (1984). *El árbol del conocimiento* [The Tree of Knowledge]. Santiago: Universitaria.

Ojeda, C. (1987). *Delirio, Realidad e Imaginación* [Delusion, Reality and Imagination]. Santiago: Universitaria.

Ojeda, C. (1993). International Classification of Diseases (CIE-10) and Diagnostic and Statistical Manual of Mental Disorders III-R: un análisis taxonómico. (CEI-10 and DSM-III: a taxonomic analysis). *Revista Chilena de Neuro-psiquiatría*, 31 (4): 373–378.

Ojeda, C. (1998). *La Presencia de lo Ausente: Ensayo sobre el Deseo* [The Presence of the Absent: an Essay on Desire]. Santiago: Cuatro Vientos.

Ojeda, C. (2003). *La Tercera Etapa* [The Third Stage]. Santiago: Cuatro Vientos.

Ojeda, C. (2006). *Martin Heidegger y el Camino Hacia el Silencio* [Martin Heidegger and the Path to Silence]. Santiago: C y C.

Orange, D. (2013). *El Desconocido Que Sufre* [The Suffering Stranger]. Santiago: Cuatro Vientos.

Ricoeur, P. (1975). *Hermenéutica y Psicoanálisis* [Hermeneutics and Psychoanalysis]. Buenos Aires: La Aurora.

Rivera, J. (2001). *Heidegger y Zubiri*. Santiago: Editorial Universitaria.

Sartre, J. -P. (1964). *Lo Imaginario* [The Imaginary]. Buenos Aires: Losada.

Sartre, J. -P. (1966). *El Ser y la Nada* [Being and Nothingness]. Buenos Aires: Losada.

Sartre, J. -P. (1988). *La Trascendencia del Ego* [The Transcendence of the Ego]. Madrid: Síntesis.

Sassenfeld, A. (2012). *Principios Clínicos de la Psicoterapia Relacional* [Clinical Principles of Relational Psychotherapy]. Santiago: Sodepsi.

Scheler, M. (1958). *La esencia de la filosofía* [The Essence of Philosophy]. Buenos Aires: Nova.

Trungpa, C. (1986). *Shambhala: La Senda Sagrada del Guerrero* [Shambhala: The Sacred Path of the Warrior]. Barcelona: Kairós.

Varela, F., & Shear, J. (2005). Metodologías en primera persona: qué, quién, cómo [Methodologies in the first person: what, who, how]. *Rev GU*, 1 (2): 148–160.

Wampold, B. (2001). *The Great Psychotherapy Debate: Models, Methods and Findings.* New York: Lawrence Erlbaum.

Zubiri, X. (1980). *Inteligencia Sentiente* [Sentient Intelligence]. Madrid: Alianza.

INDEX